WYNDHAM LEWIS

Life, Art, War

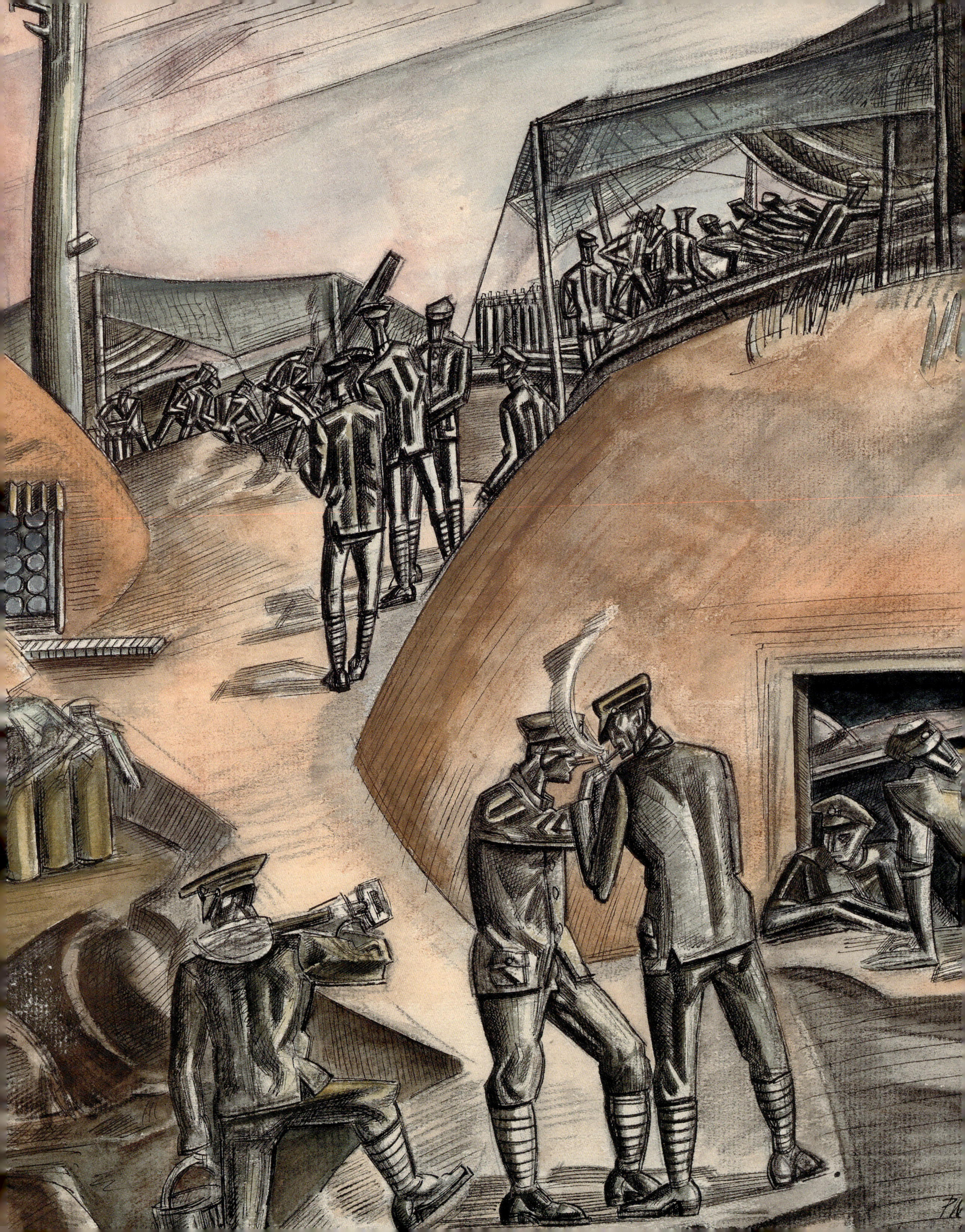

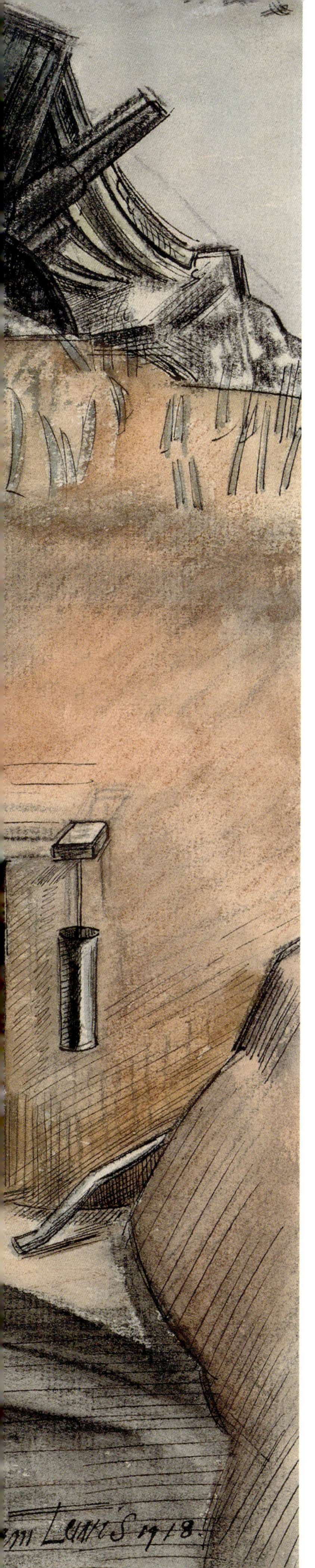

WYNDHAM LEWIS

Life, Art, War

Richard Slocombe
Preface by Paul Edwards

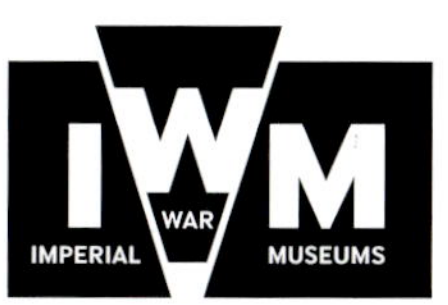

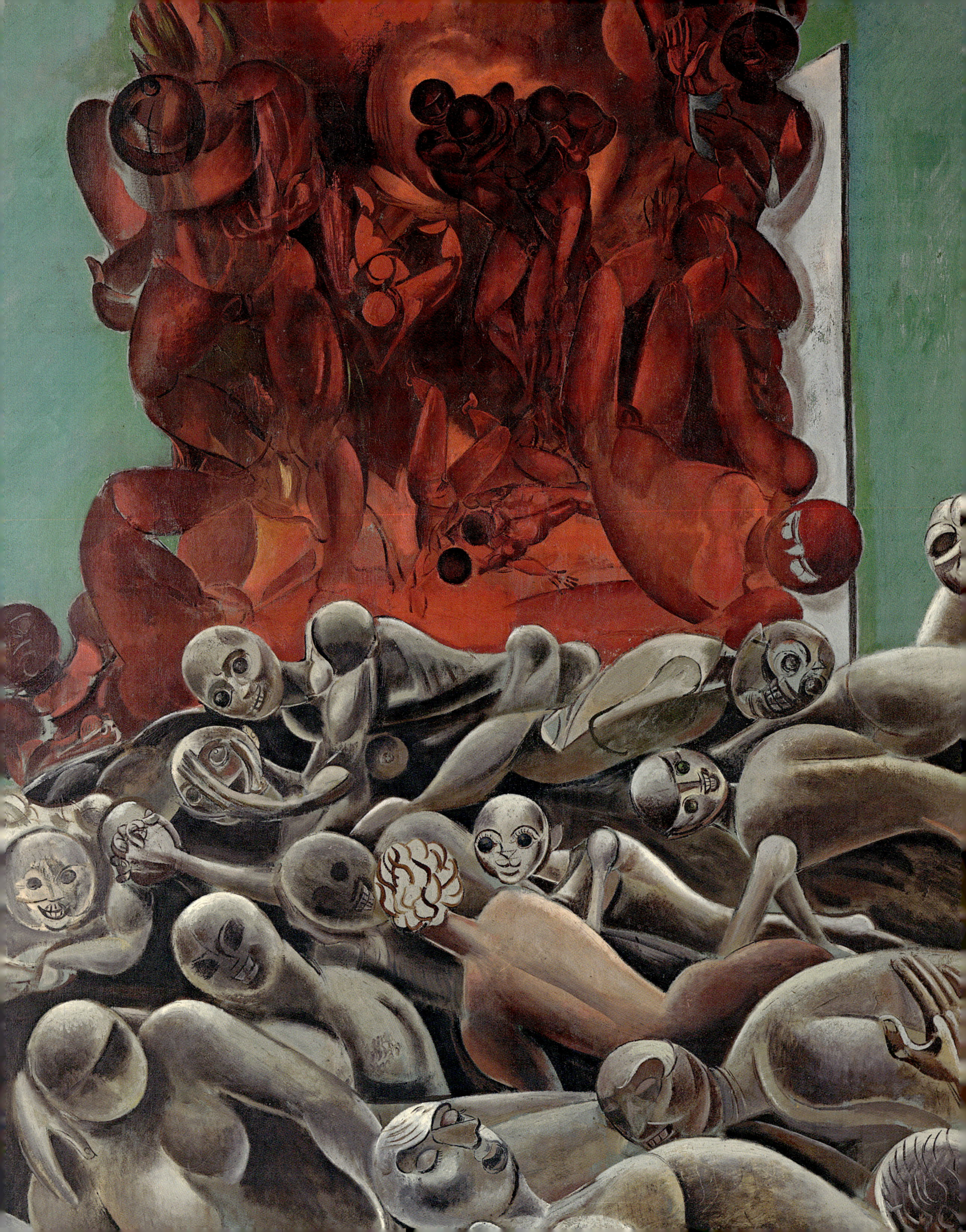

Preface: Wyndham Lewis 1882–1957   6
Paul Edwards

'Always on a War Footing': Lewis and an Era of Conflict   12
Richard Slocombe

The Plates   18

Further Reading   78
Picture Credits   79
Acknowledgements   79

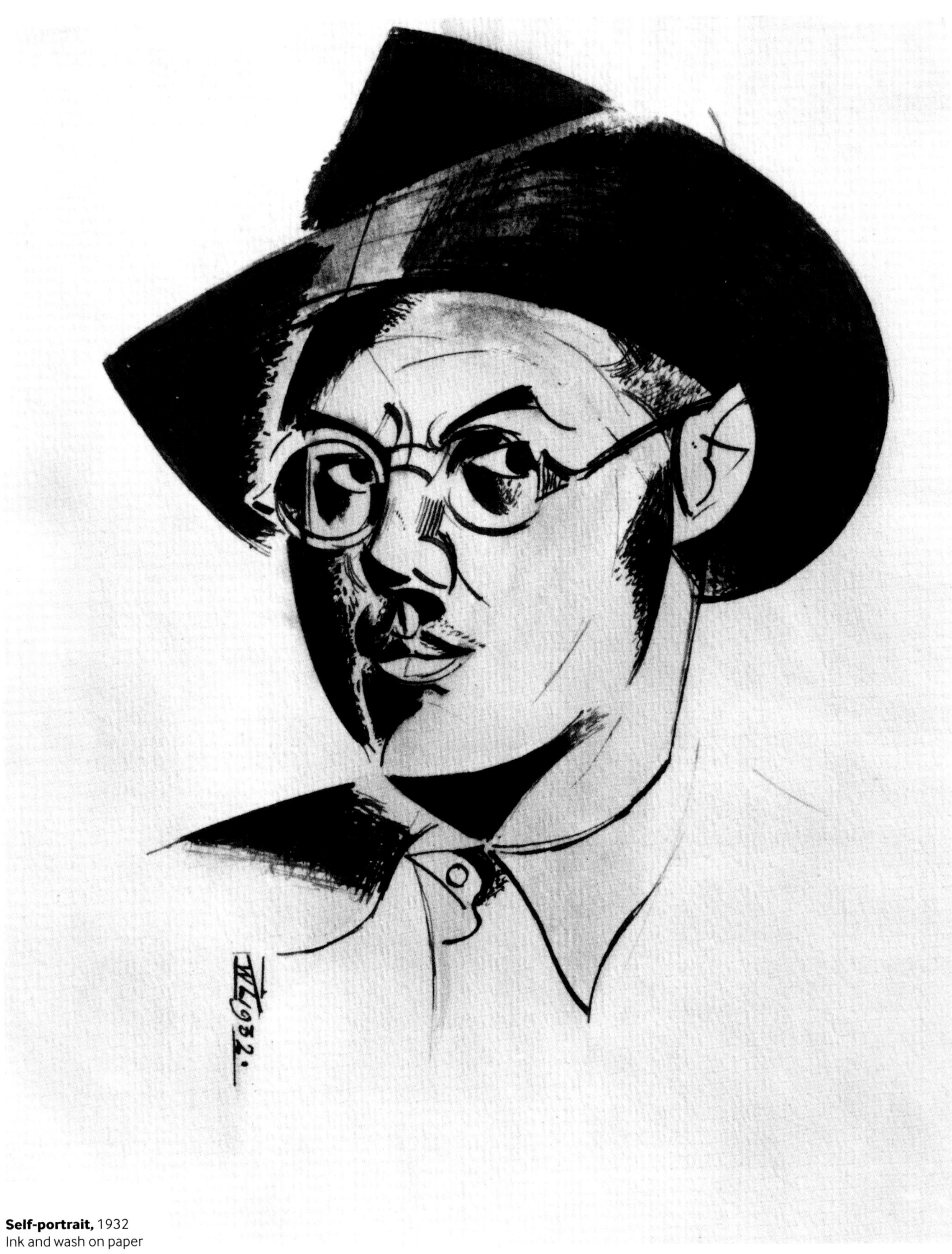

Self-portrait, 1932
Ink and wash on paper

PREFACE
Wyndham Lewis 1882–1957

Paul Edwards

For Sir Kenneth Clark, Wyndham Lewis was 'not a natural painter. He would not let himself receive sensuous impressions'. But Lewis rather disparaged painters he considered were too passive in registering their sensations. Instead, art was a kind of magic, a spell cast on reality that showed how it might be if it were arranged to reveal things our perceptual habits keep obscured from us. In one of Lewis's most alienating books, *The Childermass* (1928), ghosts try to make sense of existence in an unstable afterworld where they await endlessly deferred judgement: 'How do I come to be? Then, why am I like this?' 'What does it all mean, can you tell me?' 'What is this place we are in?' The strangeness of these surroundings turns ordinary people into philosophers.

One of the functions of art, Lewis believed, was to arouse people to a similar questioning of normality, which is why he classed his painting (along with that of Picasso and de Chirico) as 'metaphysical'. It was not meant to make us feel at home, comforted by passive 'sensuous impressions'. Neither, on the other hand, was it meant to be so gloomy as to take away all pleasure in life – the freedom, the mastery of pictorial elements exercised with such delight by the artist, were a kind of analogue for what life at its best should be: 'The great line, the creative line; the fine, exultant mass; the gaiety that snaps and clacks like a fine gut string, the sweep of great tragedy; the simple satisfaction of the surest, the completest art . . .' This was what Lewis aimed at, and sometimes achieved, especially through his linear mastery. Art was timeless in not being susceptible to 'progress'. But Lewis understood that it is also embedded in its time, that history limits our choices or suddenly widens them; that technological progress produces new ways of killing in war or, in peace, new, extended forms of self no longer determined by our biology.

Vorticism was his first deliberate effort to produce paintings that embodied the 'new egos' inhabiting the modern city, sharing its potential for varied and contradictory life. The style developed from his 1912–13 *Timon of Athens* portfolio (overleaf), which showed Timon enmeshed (in this case tragically) in the material matrix from which he was constructed. The human figure is deconstructed and redistributed around the picture plane in machine-like forms that are simultaneously architectonic and diagrammatic. Textures mimic the grimy blacks and reds of railway yards or the cheap coloured surfaces in A.B.C. restaurants. The Vorticist pictures are a magical equivalent of life in the modern city – or 'pictorial spells', as Lewis called them – designed to illuminate a reconstitution of our being in the world. Immediately after the First World War, Lewis proposed that this vision should become real in a kind of zestful architecture based on Vorticist abstraction (as it now seems in such buildings as Daniel Libeskind's). It is appropriate that Lewis's work should be exhibited in Libeskind's IWM of the North. Vorticism now also seems prophetic of war, as do the titles of Lewis's lost paintings, *Plan of War* and *Slow Attack*. But when war came, less than a month after the launch of Vorticism, Lewis did not welcome it, and his experience as an artillery officer at Passchendaele gave him a hatred of war that influenced nearly all his subsequent work.

When a new architecture for a new humanity did not arrive after the war, he satirised a shell-shocked society in grotesque effigies: 'tyros' (pp 44–45). The pictures also satirised the complacency of the classical revival and development of 'Purism' in French painting. It is typical of Lewis's complexity that the incisive, zestful but sometimes pitiless line of his drawing in 1919–22 (such as *Nude 1*, page 46) should derive from classicism, however. In *Mrs Workman* (1923; private collection), for example, he showed his mastery of the Ingres mode he officially rejected. It is often thought that Lewis abandoned abstraction after his war-art had brought him back to figuration. His abstract and semi-abstract works of 1921–27 show this is too simple, and drawings like *Archimedes Reconnoitring the Enemy Fleet* (opposite), with its lyrical interleaved planes and intricate indecipherable hieroglyphs, show him as one of the most advanced painters in post-war Europe.

It is exasperating for admirers of Lewis's visual art that by 1924 (visually, a barren year), painting had become a spare-time activity. He put his energy into writing – political theory, literary and cultural criticism, philosophical criticism, satire and fantasy, three issues of a new magazine (*The Enemy*), two new and two revised books of fiction, and four books of non-fiction, all published in the years 1926–30. All, in a way, are responses to the First World War, attempts to understand the ideologies that made wars possible. Lewis found most of his contemporaries to be ignorantly collusive with the ideology he was warning against – Bergsonian 'time-philosophy'. The books are intended also to lead the West away from war towards fulfilment of the revolution inherent in modernist culture. There is much of value in

the books, but also something deeply mistaken in them, for they precede an endorsement of dictatorship and (in 1931) of Hitler as a bulwark against a new war. Only late in 1937, after several pro-appeasement books, did Lewis admit to having been 'much-deceived'.

Visual art was for Lewis the antithesis of the massive negation in his writing. Hence the many Creation Myths he painted. He opposed cyclical theories of history in his books, but *Bagdad* (1927–28; Tate), with its Yeatsian 'winding stair' of history, leads us upwards to an idyllic garden city that repeats an ancient utopia. But optimism was difficult to sustain during the 1930s. A different kind of historical repetition characterises *The Surrender of Barcelona* (pp 62–63), an apparently festive patchwork of shapes and colours: banner-bedraped towers, warm reds and yellows offset by lyrical blues. Closer inspection reveals, within its interstices, armoured figures and the

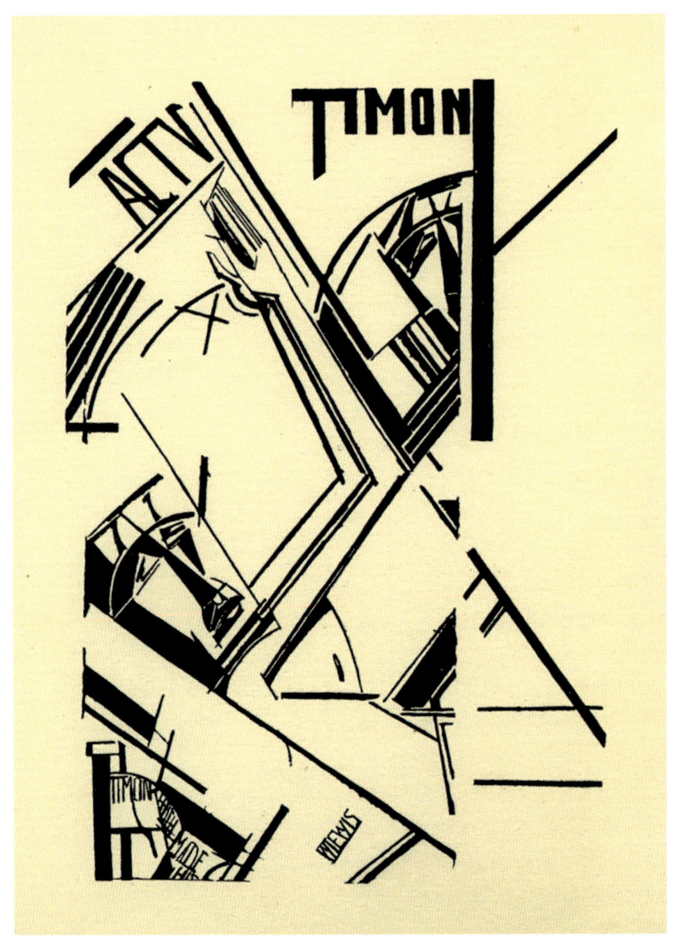

**Timon of Athens Act V. Print from
the Timon of Athens portfolio,**
London, 1913

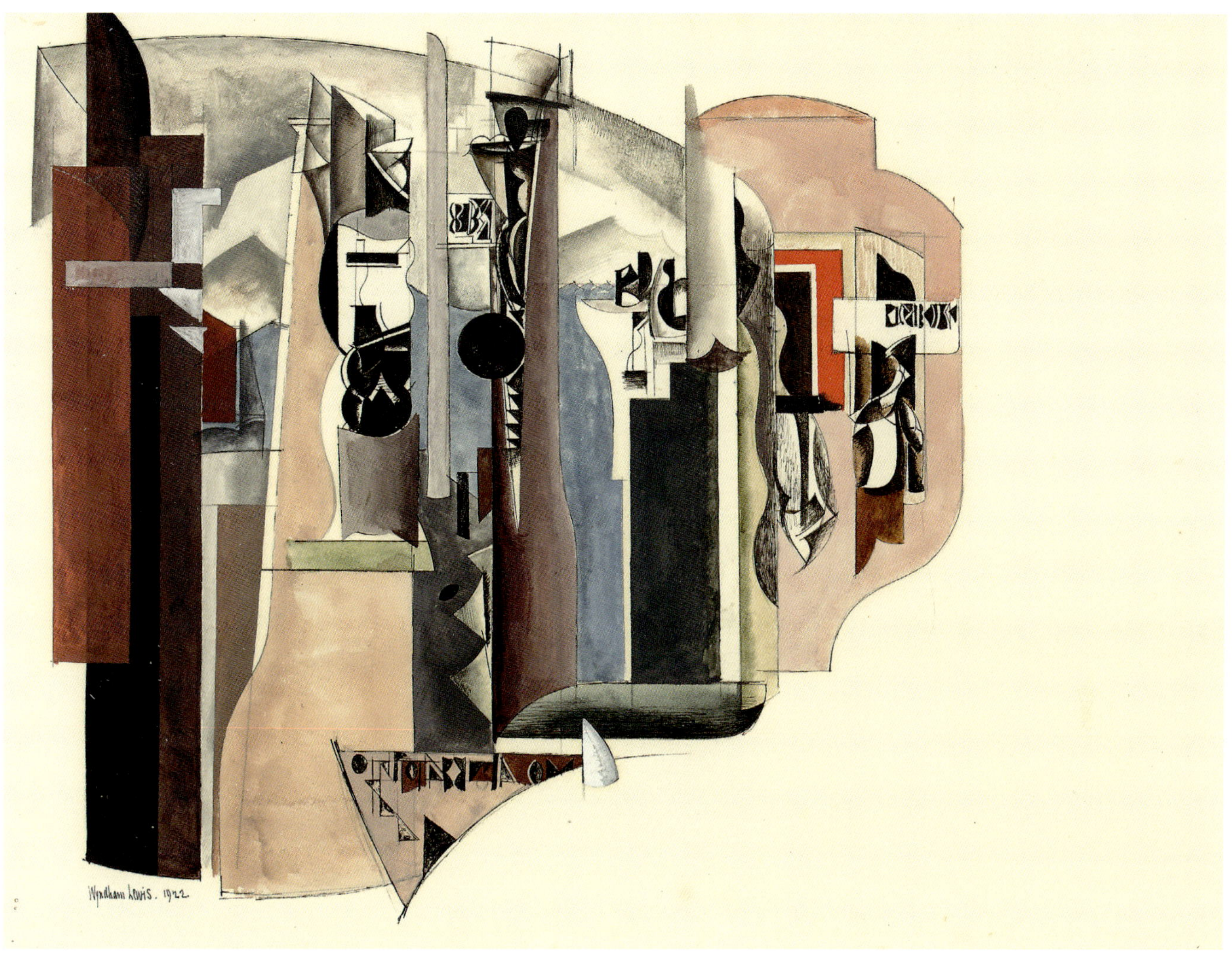

Archimedes, Reconnoitring the Fleet, 1922
Pencil, ink, watercolour and gouache on paper. 33 x 47.5 cm
Private collection

violence they inflict, symbolised by the gibbeted corpse at the lower centre — a scene that was to materialise three years after the painting was started, when Barcelona fell to Franco's forces.

If Lewis's writing in the 1920s aspired to anatomise the whole of Western culture, in the 1930s his painting became the vehicle of a comprehensive vision of life, encompassing social satire (*Two Beach Babies;* pp 60–61), cultural diffusion (*Inca with Birds;* pp 58–59), sickness and convalescence (*The Tank in the Clinic;* pp 68–69), a life of pure spirit (*Three Veiled Figures;* overleaf), or an afterlife of Renaissance energies from which spirit has been banished (*Inferno;* pp 72–73). This last was the centrepiece of Lewis's 1937 exhibition of this 'series' (as he called it) of paintings. The current exhibition is the first chance in

nearly 40 years for a British audience to see it 'in the flesh' and feel its unsettling power.

Rarely seen, too, is the portrait of T S Eliot (pp 74–75), rejected by the Royal Academy in 1938, reworked and then sold to Durban Art Gallery. Lewis knew war was returning, and his mind turned to commemoration of his modernist associates — Eliot, Pound (p.47) and (in a memoir, *Blasting and Bombardiering*) Hulme and Joyce. The portraits, along with earlier ones, and the 'red' portraits of Lewis's wife (pp 64–65), are among his finest achievements.

Expecting fruitful portrait commissions, Lewis turned his back on a European civilisation destroying itself and sailed to North America, with his wife and their dog, in September 1939. But the hand-to-mouth existence they

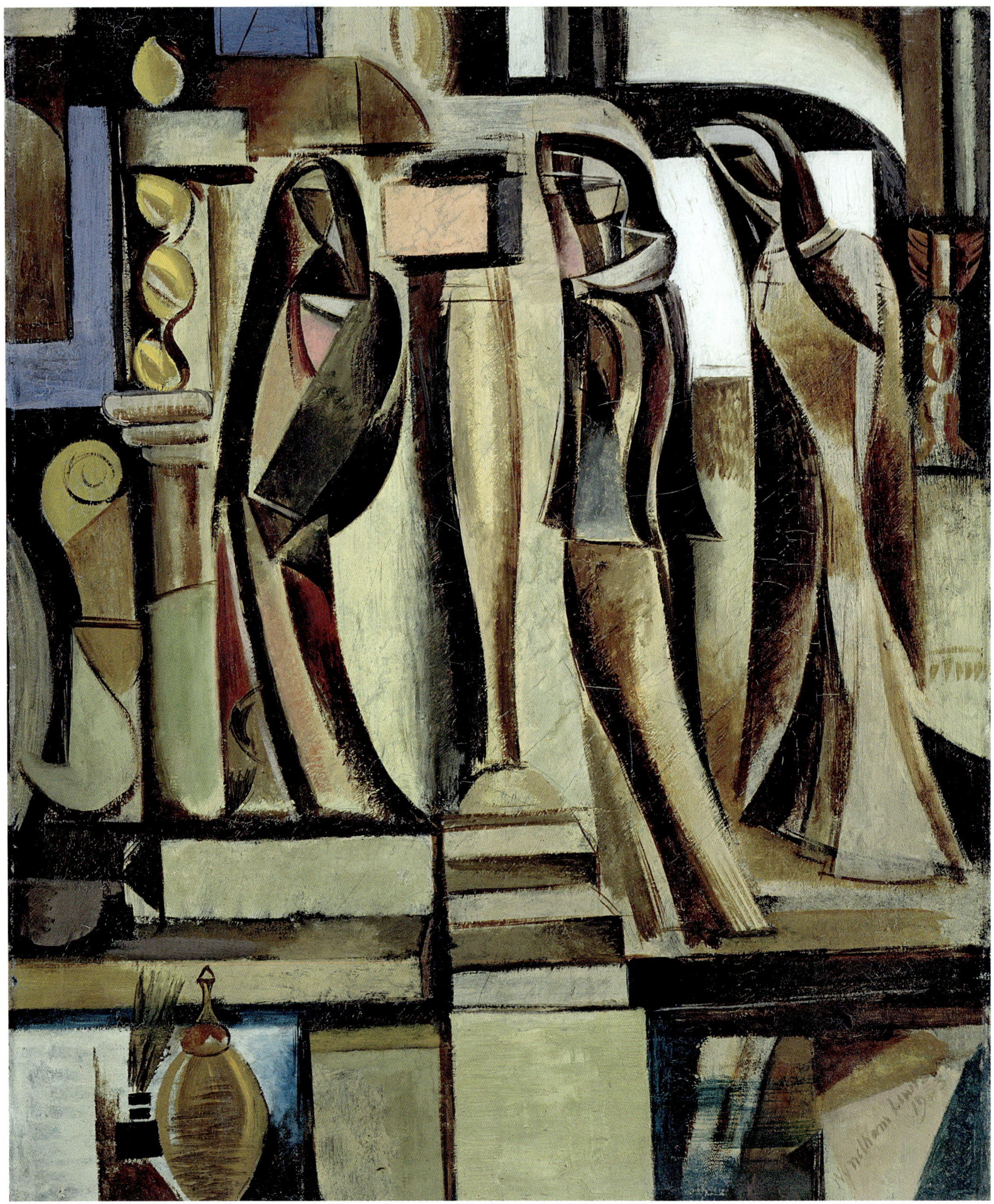

Three Veiled Figures, 1933
Oil on canvas, 51 x 43 cm
Leeds Art Gallery: LMG130792

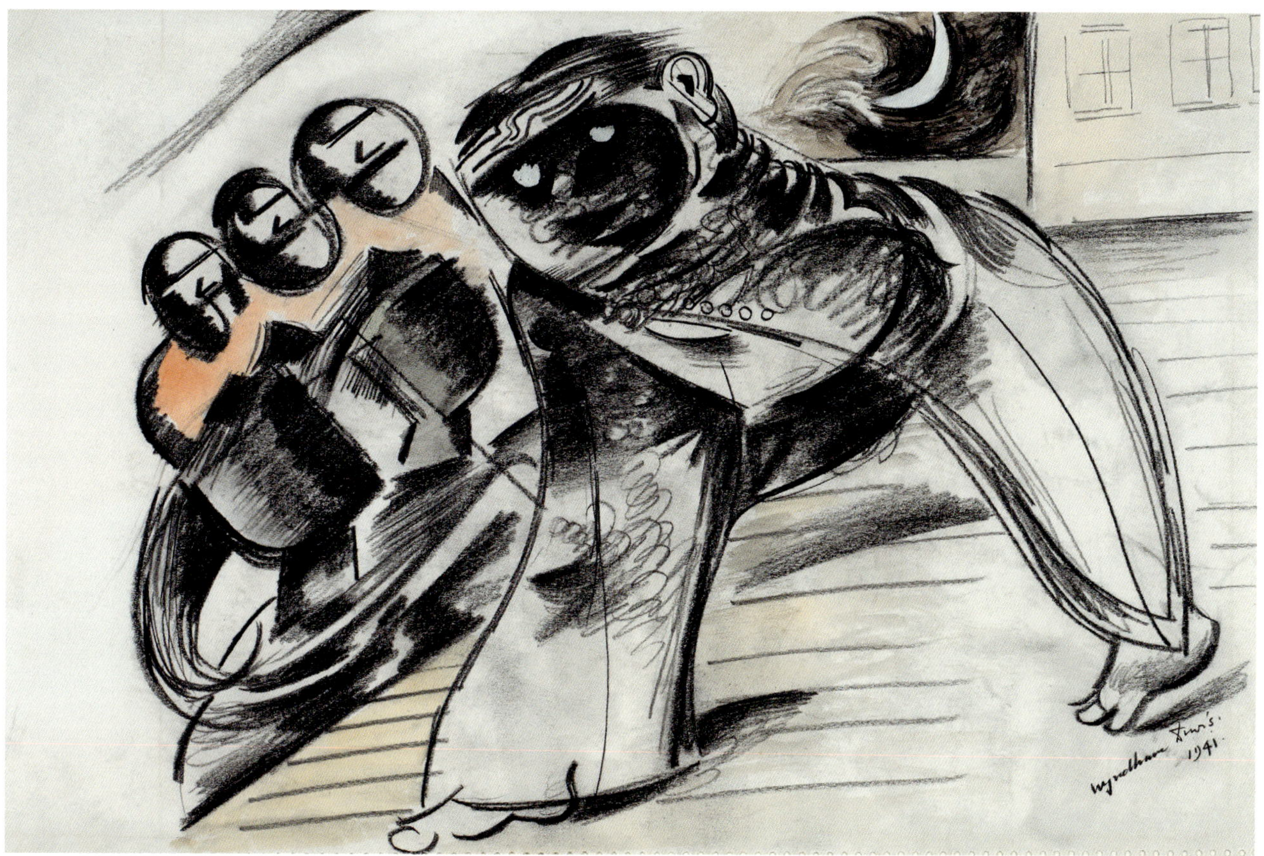

Armless Man on Stage, 1949
Chalk and wash on paper, 44 x 28.5 cm
Wyndham Lewis Memorial Trust: LD.2010.XX.6

endured there was a nightmare. Their life in a Toronto hotel features in the 1954 novel, *Self Condemned,* which T S Eliot called 'a book of almost unbearable spiritual agony', and which Pound thought should win the Nobel Prize. While in Toronto, Lewis noticed the beginnings of damage to his eyesight, which by 1951 would lead to virtual blindness and end his career both as a painter and a (surprisingly positive) art critic for the *Listener.* The anguish of this, and of exile during a war whose effects he had not really escaped, gave rise to a last crowning achievement in his visual art in 1941–42 – fantastic imaginative pastels and watercolours depicting biological 'creation', bathers delighting in water, expressionistic transpositions of the horrors of war in scenes like *Armless Man on Stage* (above), and an anguished series of four *Small Crucifixions* (one now in a private collection; the others part of The Wyndham Lewis Memorial Trust collection).

Returning to Britain in 1945, Lewis achieved a measure of recognition, especially after his *The Human Age*, a continuation of *The Childermass*, was broadcast in dramatised form on the BBC Third programme, and the Tate Gallery produced what was almost a retrospective, *Wyndham Lewis and Vorticism*, in 1956, not long before his death. It was a gesture they have never repeated, and Lewis's work remains comparatively little-seen. His political misjudgements and his own 'enemy' stance made him too many enemies, no doubt. But when asked by Mervyn Levy at the opening of the Tate exhibition about one particular 'enemy', he replied 'There is only one enemy – oneself'. Within a year, Levy records, Lewis was dead.

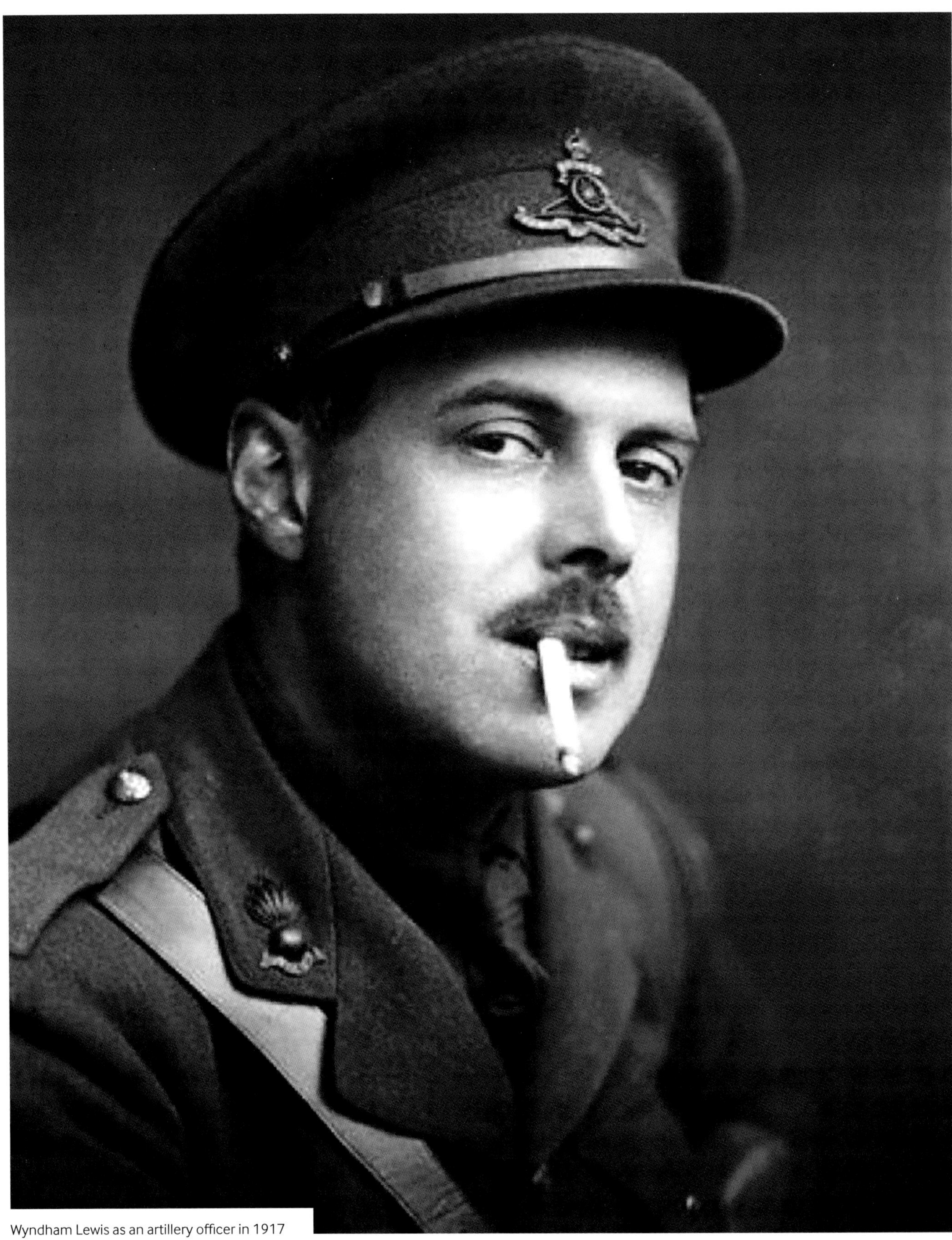

Wyndham Lewis as an artillery officer in 1917

'ALWAYS ON A WAR FOOTING'
Lewis and an era of conflict

Richard Slocombe

[Lewis] was always on a war footing; he believed others were likewise disposed … War played, I think, a considerable part in his imaginative life: he occasionally used military terms to describe his own operations, offensive or defensive, and he alluded more than once to his belonging by birth 'to a military caste'.

John Rothenstein, *1966, p.42*

These words of John Rothenstein, one-time Director of the Tate and long-term Lewis champion, capture the common view of an aggressive, antagonistic and bellicose Wyndham Lewis. The reality was, of course, more complex — this most independent of thinkers was prone to wilful contradiction and deliberate provocation. It is without doubt though that Lewis's life, attitudes and art were impacted by the most violent and chaotic period in recent human history; an era that encompassed two world wars, Bolshevik revolution, the rise of Stalin and fascism, the Spanish Civil War, the Nazi Holocaust and the emergent nuclear age. His works were suffused with the key doctrines and philosophies of the modern epoch, from Bergsonian and Nietzchean 'process philosophy' to the existential angst of the post-45 era. Lewis's own critical writing, acerbic satire and

social commentary were notorious, assailing not only the cream of British literary society but also major figures of the day, from Chaplin to Hitler.

The shadow of war was present from the very beginning. Lewis's errant father was a former US cavalry officer and Civil War veteran — hence the talk of 'a military caste'. Lewis subsequently grew up in a Britain riven with political, class and generational discord; a situation played out across all Europe's major powers, edging each towards internecine conflict in 1914. By founding the avant-garde Vorticist group and its polemical, *BLAST*, in June 1914 (see overleaf), Lewis was a high-profile embodiment of the restless iconoclasm of Britain's educated youth on the eve of the First World War. Indeed, the war for the likes of D H Lawrence and C R W Nevinson offered a harsh tonic for a moribund society. For his part, Lewis rejected the notion of a 'regenerative war' and regarded the First World War as the terrible, but logical,

No. 1. June 20th, 1914.

BLAST

Edited by WYNDHAM LEWIS.

REVIEW OF THE GREAT ENGLISH VORTEX.

2/6 Published Quarterly.
10/6 Yearly Subscription.

London :
JOHN LANE,
The Bodley Head.
New York : John Lane Company.
Toronto : Bell & Cockburn.

Blast: Review of the Great English Vortex, 20 June 1914
Titlepage of the first issue

MANIFESTO.

I.

1 Beyond Action and Reaction we would establish ourselves.

2 We start from opposite statements of a chosen world. Set up violent structure of adolescent clearness between two extremes.

3 We discharge ourselves on both sides.

4 We fight first on one side, then on the other, but always for the SAME cause, which is neither side or both sides and ours.

5 Mercenaries were always the best troops.

6 We are Primitive Mercenaries in the Modern World.

7 Our Cause is NO-MAN'S.

8 We set Humour at Humour's throat. Stir up Civil War among peaceful apes.

9 We only want Humour if it has fought like Tragedy.

10 We only want Tragedy if it can clench its side-muscles like hands on it's belly, and bring to the surface a laugh like a bomb.

Blast: Review of the Great English Vortex, 20 June 1914
Double-page spread entititled 'Manifesto'

outcome of the philosopher Henri Bergson's notion of Creative Evolution. This urged humans to embrace a universal 'life force' and submit to the impulses of the animal kingdom. Drawings such as the 1914 *Combat No.2* (p.36), therefore, offer an image of a humanity reduced to mechanical urges to either fight or mate.

The First World War was the nemesis of Vorticism, its followers scattered by service or killed in the fighting. Lewis himself underwent a hiatus from artistic activity while serving as a subaltern with the 330th Siege Battery of the Royal Garrison Artillery. The art he subsequently created, both privately and as an official war artist for the Canadians and the British from 1917, was much changed from his Vorticist abstraction. He insisted that the stylised figuration adopted in his drawings was 'a direct, ready formula to give interpretation to what I took part in in France', motivated by a desire 'to do with a pencil and brush what story-tellers like Tchekov or Stendhal did in their books'. However, saying also that

he had 'abandoned those vexing diagrams by which he puzzled and annoyed' meant no return to Vorticism, but instead a greater regard for subject matter and narrative, culminating in a wartime magnum opus, *A Battery Shelled* (pp 42–43).

A Battery Shelled fulfilled an ambition to synthesise modernist sensibility with the grand tradition of history painting. Lewis achieved this feat again eighteen years later with his impressive *The Surrender of Barcelona* (pp 62–63), a partial homage to Diego Velasquez's *The Surrender of Breda* (1634–35). Begun in 1936, three hundred years after the Velasquez masterpiece, its production coincided with the outbreak of the Spanish Civil War — though Lewis was guarded about any immediate association with the conflict. As with all Lewis's historical subjects of the 1930s it concerned violent conquest, and seemed to reflect and anticipate current and future conflicts. Coinciding with this was the publication of *Blasting and Bombardiering* (1937),

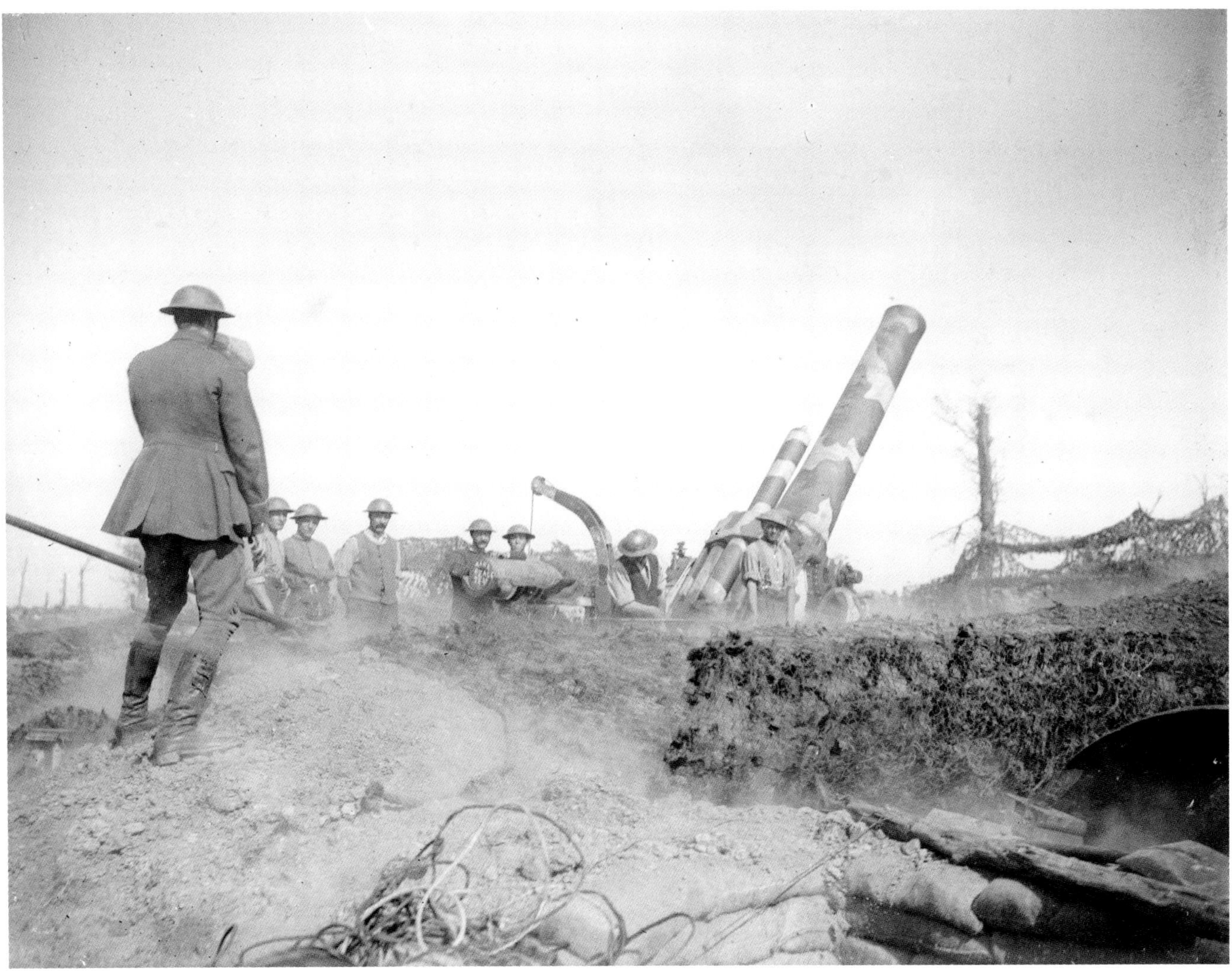

104th Siege Battery, Royal Garrison Artillery, 24 September 1917, with a camouflage-painted 12-inch
Howitzer. Zillebeke, Battle of the Menin Road Ridge. IWM Q 7808

Lewis's timely autobiography of his career prior to and
during First World War. Besides detailing his exuberant
pre-war years and the ensuing disillusion of the war, the
spectre of future conflict loomed large over its pages,
with Lewis – the veteran – cautioning: 'There is for me
no good war and bad war. There is only bad war.'

Lewis's resentment towards the First World War
was acute and engrained; it robbed him of his friend
Henri Gaudier-Brezska, denied him his most productive
years and, most painfully, took his beloved mother.
The strain of war, Lewis was convinced, caused her

premature death in 1920. His own experiences serving
at Messines Ridge and Passchendaele in 1917 would
colour his subsequent outlook and expectations, and
the 'deliberately invented scenes' of the Western
Front would inspire some of his most compelling and
disturbing art and literature.

In the 1930s a personal crusade to prevent future war
saw Lewis embark on a period of political writing, the
ill-judged conclusions of which was to have dire personal
consequences. Already preferring authoritarian power
over democracy (disdained as rule by the 'herd'), a chief

concern of Lewis was the perceived 'left-wing orthodoxy' of a blinkered British cultural elite. Virulent anti-communism blinded him to the evils of fascism. In 1931 his infamous essay, *Hitler*, portrayed the Nazi leader as a 'man of peace' and a barrier to Soviet incursion in Europe. Lewis backed his position five years later in *Left Wings over Europe*, urging appeasement of Hitler and Mussolini and dismissing, like many others, warnings to the contrary from Winston Churchill as war-mongering. Similarly, in *Count Your Dead – They Are Alive!*, Lewis excused the actions of General Franco in the Spanish Civil War as necessary to resist communism.

Too late then was Lewis's trip to Nazi Germany in 1937, which exposed the true nature of the regime. Hastily recanting his earlier pronouncements, he published *The Jews: Are they Human?*, a sincere but ham-fisted denouncement of anti-Semitism, and *The Hitler Cult and How it Will End* (1939). In this, Lewis derided the Führer as a deluded romantic confronted by realities he could not understand.

Yet the damage was done. For Lewis's detractors his association with Nazism was unforgivable, and his reputation has never recovered. He faced further criticism for his apparent desertion of Britain for Canada at the outbreak of the Second World War. Intended as a fresh start abroad after the controversial rejection of his portrait of T S Eliot by the Royal Academy in 1938, Lewis found life in the 'stony desert' of New York and the 'sanctimonious icebox' of Toronto no more conducive. In poor health and facing destitution, he was cast a lifeline in 1943 by Britain's official war art scheme. However, Lewis's commissioned painting, *A Canadian War Factory*, proved problematic. Afflicted with self-doubt and indecision he changed his approach twice, so that by his return to Britain in August 1945 it was still unfinished.

Lewis returned to a country exhausted by war and in the grip of austerity, a state of affairs he powerfully evoked in his collection of literary sketches, *Rotting Hill*. Despite approaching blindness, this final period of Lewis's life was perhaps his most stable. As art critic for the BBC's cultural weekly, the *Listener*, he championed a new generation of British artists, including Francis Bacon, Michael Ayrton, Barbara Hepworth and John Minton, and even advocated state-subsidised arts on a par with the newly formed National Health Service. In 1951 the BBC commissioned Lewis to complete his Dantesque afterlife trilogy, *The Human Age*, initially begun in 1928 with *The Childermass*. The three volumes conjured a nightmare fantasy world of corporate consumption, compliant masses and a hell operated by a dapper devil, Sammael. Undoubtedly Lewis's hellish imagery was derived from his experience of the Western Front, and later by images of the Nazi concentration camps – though, as a whole, *The Human Age* was a response to the Cold War and the capitalism of the post-war, which the author believed would lead inevitably to a future nuclear world war.

Thankfully, this is a prediction from this most astute of modern minds that has until now proven wrong.

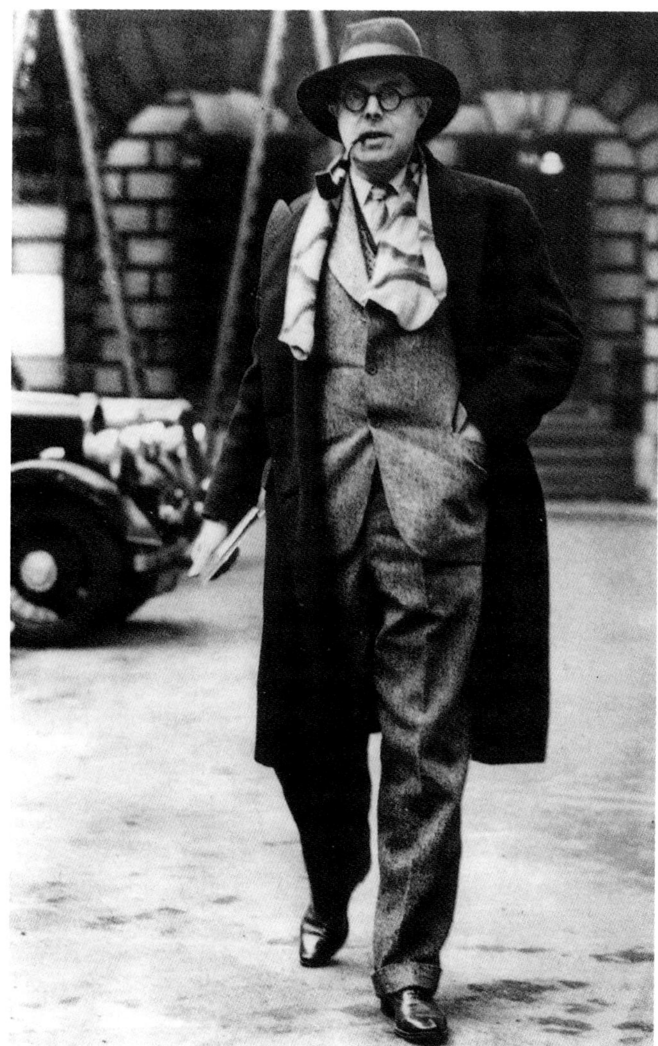

Wyndham Lewis outside the Royal Academy on press day of the 1938 RA summer show (he reviewed the show, from which his portrait of T S Eliot had been controversially excluded)

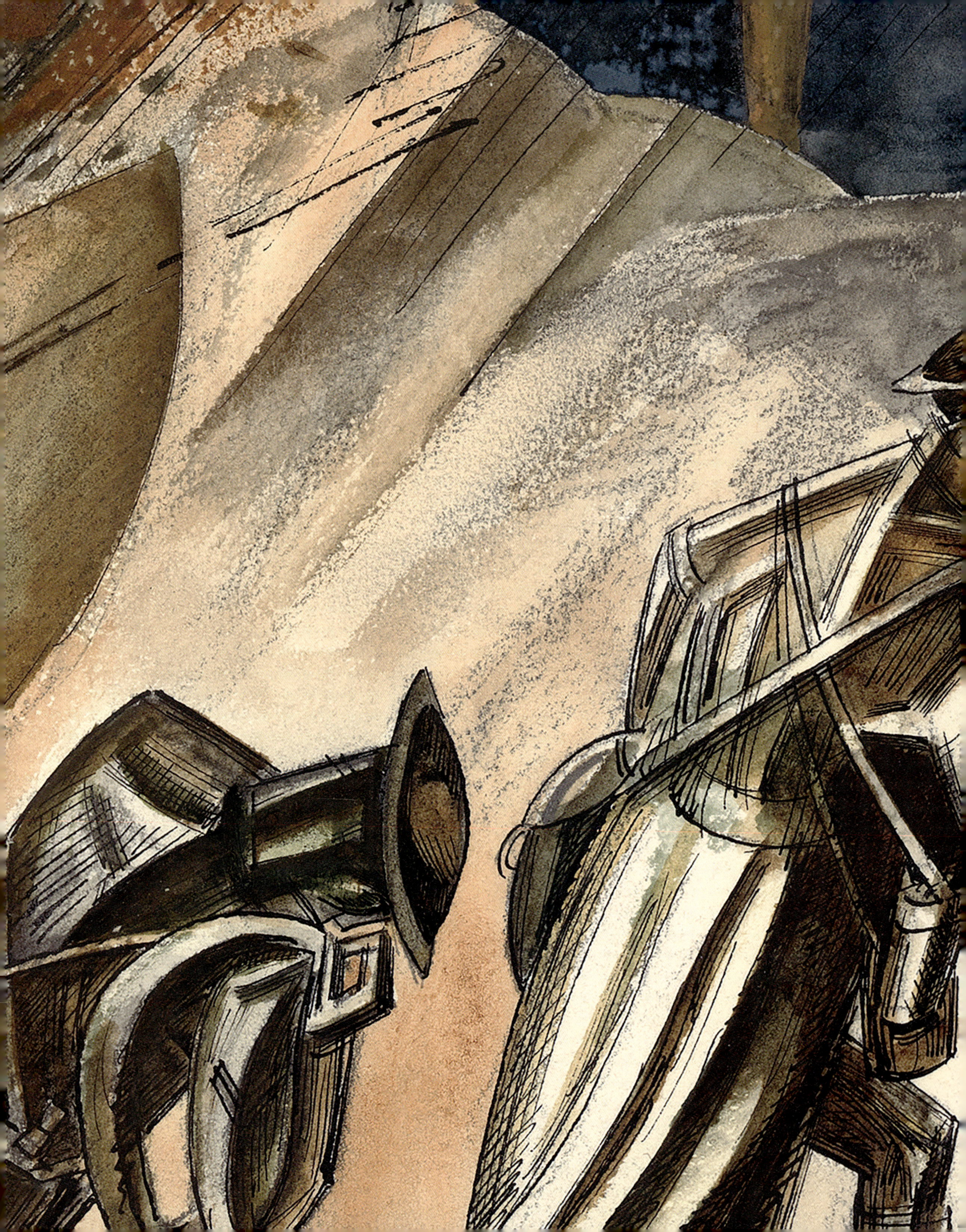

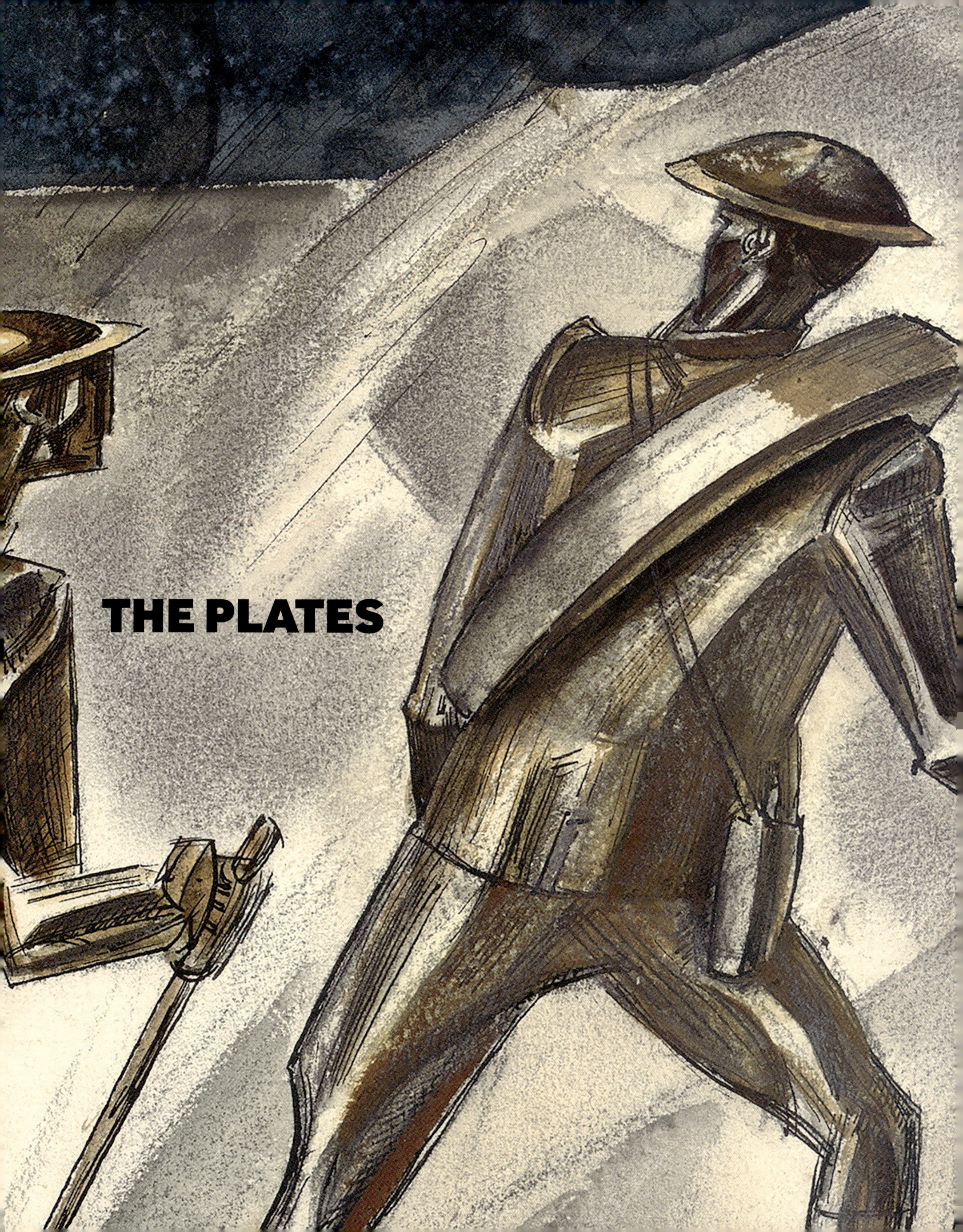
THE PLATES

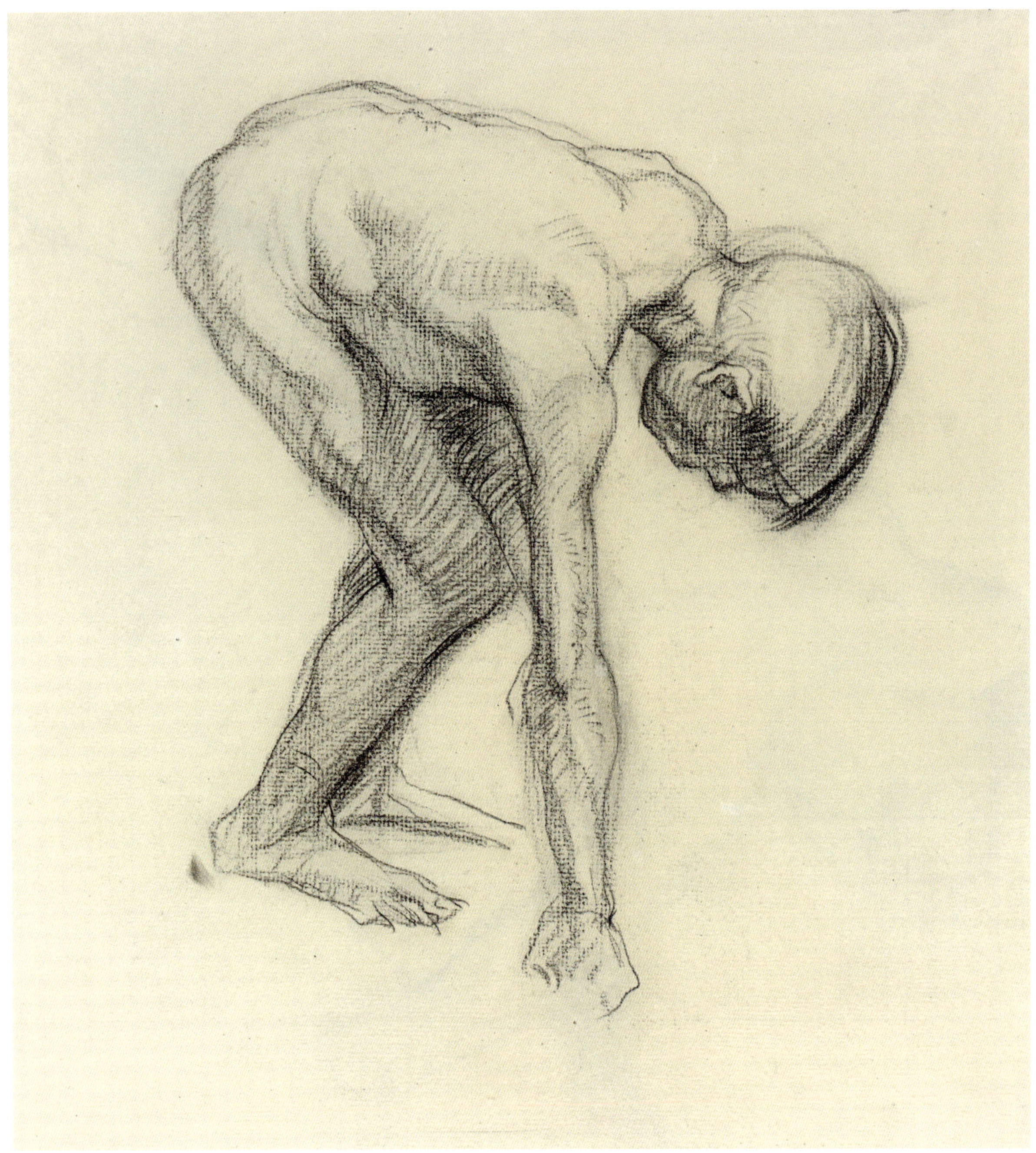

STANDING MALE NUDE, 1901
Pencil on paper, 52.8 x 32.9 cm
UCL Art Museum, London: 6040

STOOPING NUDE CHILD, 1900
Pencil on paper, 34.5 x 29 cm
UCL Art Museum, London: 6003

These two life studies date from Lewis's brief time at the Slade School of Art. Both show an absorption of the analytical High Renaissance-inspired methods of the Slade's drawing professor, Henry Tonks, while at the same time revealing Lewis's natural gift for expressive line.

Lewis's artistic interest developed as a schoolboy at Rugby. However, this, combined with his poor academic record and distaste for the school's traditions and pupil hierarchies, contributed to a sense of alienation. He entered the Slade in 1898 and quickly gained a reputation as its best draughtsman since Augustus John. Even so, Lewis was critical of the school's teaching methods and was eventually expelled for poor attendance in 1901. These two studies provided a glimpse of Lewis's future priorities, especially in the development of the disciplined linear figuration that was characteristic of his mature career.

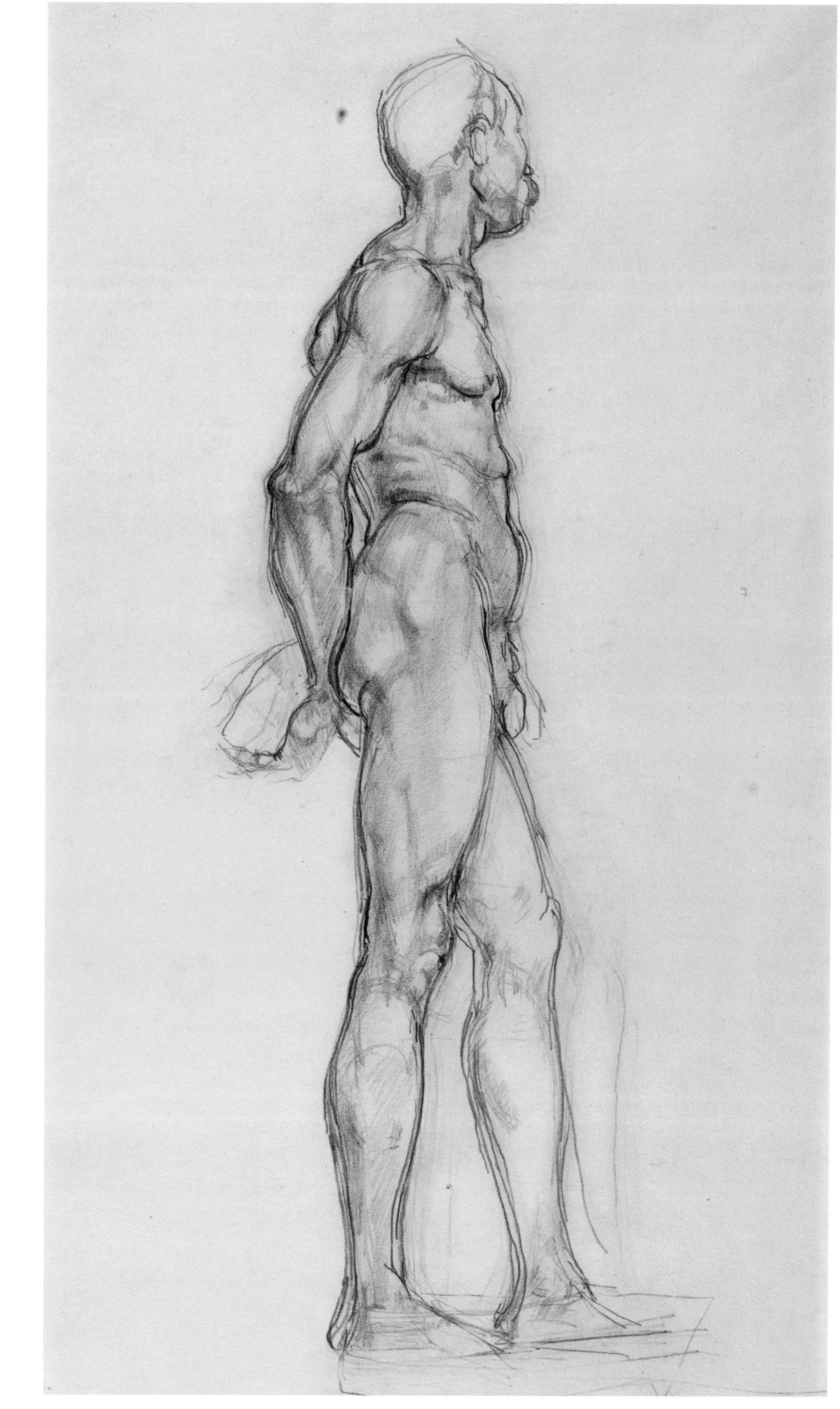

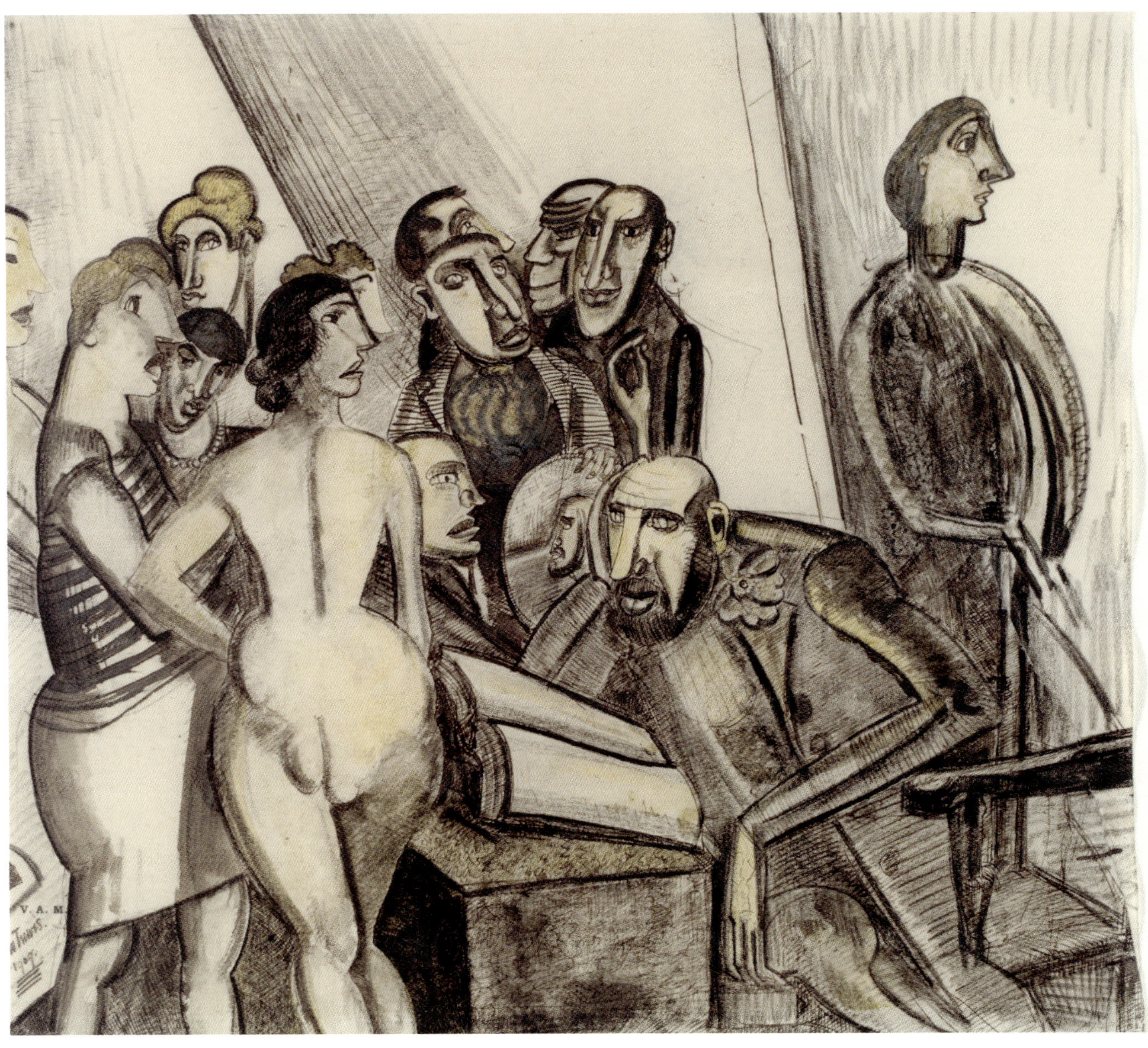

THE THEATRE MANAGER, 1909
Pen and ink, watercolour, 29.5 x 31.5 cm
Victoria and Albert Museum, London: E.3779–1919

Lewis's friendship with the artists Augustus John and Harold Gilman influenced him to commit to art in 1909, having toyed with becoming a poet. His early works often expressed a dislocation from society, identifying with lonely, marginalised figures or picturing sardonic low-life scenes, such as his drawing *The Theatre Manager*.

The choice of a theatrical subject was typical of Gilman's Camden Town Group, which drew inspiration from the urban working-class scenes of Walter Sickert (1860–1942). Lewis was admitted as a member in 1911. However, the drawing's grotesquely caricatured actors were deliberately provocative, and other drawings by Lewis in a similiar style drew criticism from within the Camden Town Group when shown at the group's inaugural exhibition the same year.

Despite this, *The Theatre Manager* had a serious intent – the eponymous theatre manager and his motley troupe representing the relationship between the individual and the group. The isolation and anguish of the manager, as he wrestles with the script and his unpromising actors, is emphasised by his facing opposite his unassuming charges. His reflection caught in a mirror held by one of the actors stresses the dichotomy of the private inner self and that of the projected persona, an obsession that would dominate much of Lewis's life.

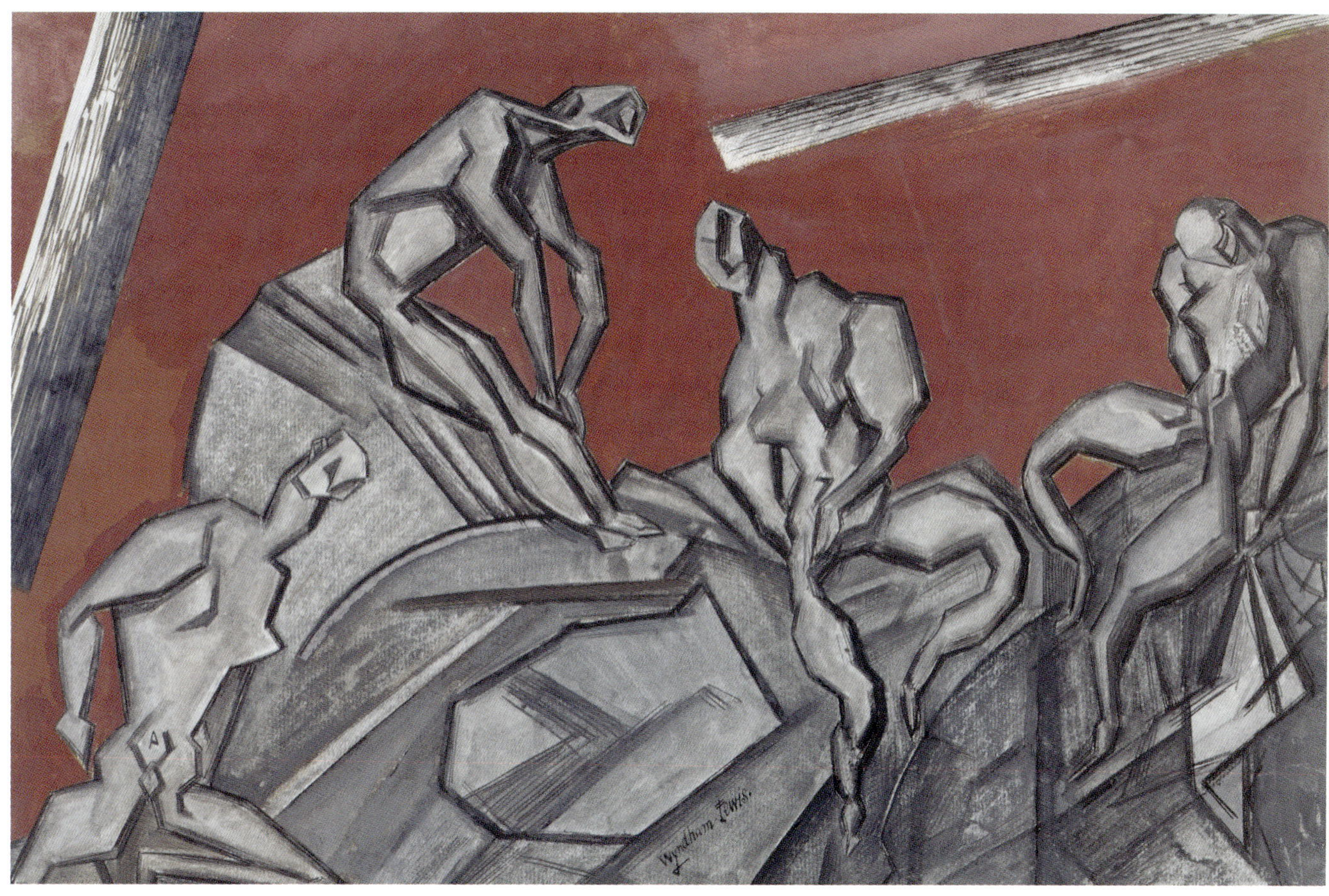

SUNSET AMONG THE MICHELANGELOS, c.1912
Pen & ink and gouache, 32.3 x 47.8 cm
Victoria and Albert Museum, London: E.3759.1919

Lewis's early experimental drawing, *Sunset among the Michelangelos*, demonstrates his willingness
to adopt, transcend and even parody prevalent modern styles. It visualises the decline of one artistic
tradition and the emergence of another. The 'Michelangelos' of the title was meant as an ironic
reference to Lewis's Slade school teaching and the Renaissance-inspired instruction of its drawing
professor, Henry Tonks. This is now superseded by the awkward Cubist figures appearing from a rocky
landscape, signalling the ascent of Pablo Picasso and the modernists of the School of Paris.

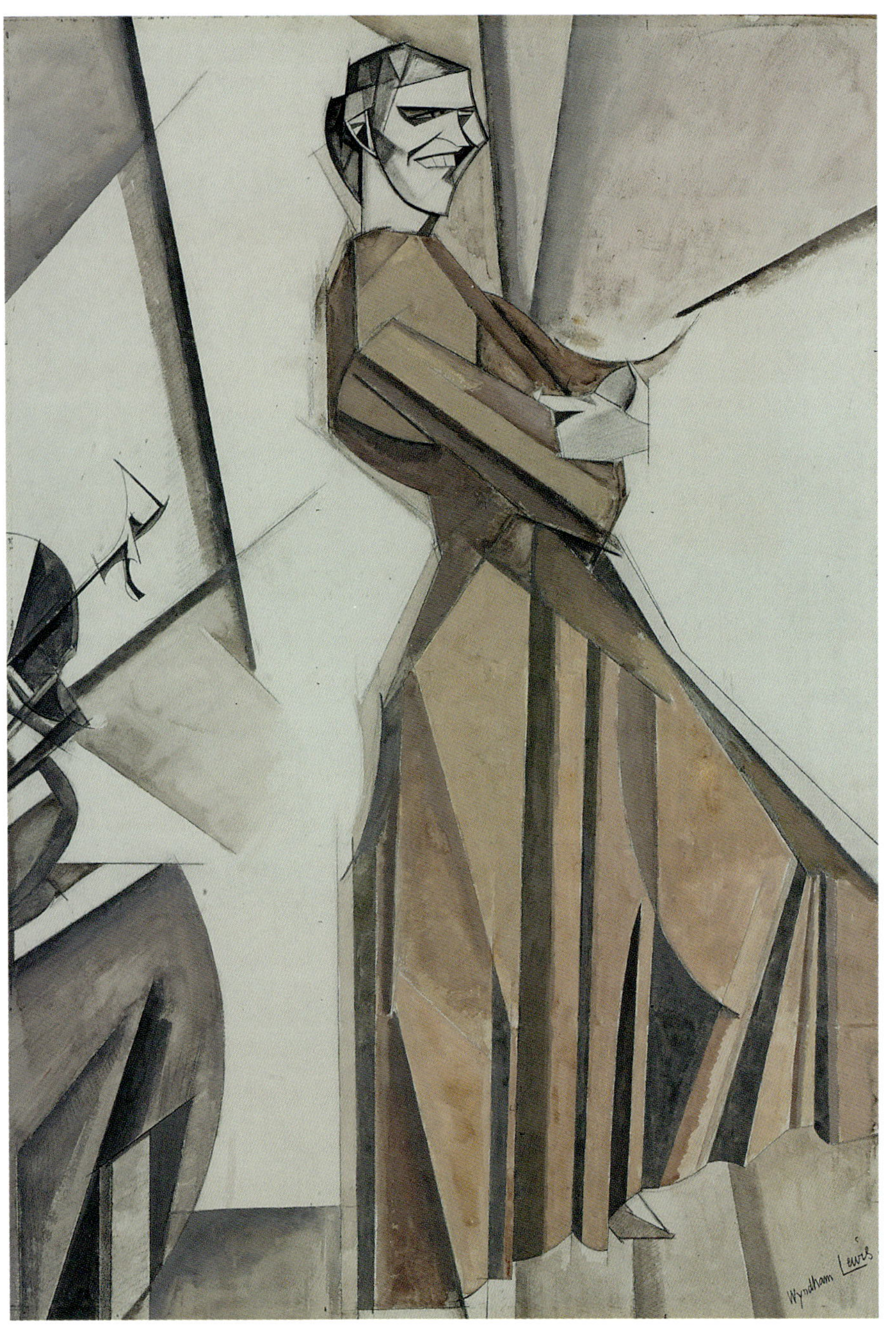

SMILING WOMAN ASCENDING A STAIR, c.1911–12
Charcoal and gouache, 95 x 65 cm
Private collection

Lewis's *Smiling Woman Ascending a Stair* was a dramatic early foray into Cubism. Its title suggests inspiration from Marcel Duchamp's iconic *Nude Descending a Staircase, No. 2* (1912), but it was most likely influenced by Augustus John's *Woman Smiling* (1908–9). Lewis's often fractious relationship with John is reflected in *Smiling Woman*, which seems to be both tribute and riposte to the latter's portrait. On the one-hand the drawing incorporates the long russet gypsy gown of John's subject, but in its harsh angularity and the rictus grin of his woman Lewis seems to announce the demise of John's gentler Post-Impressionism, replaced by the Cubism of a younger generation.

    Lewis's *Smiling Woman* is Kate Lechmere, a fellow painter, his some time lover and the financial backer for his Rebel Art Centre in 1913. She became the subject of a brief but bitter love rivalry between Lewis and the philosopher T E Hulme. This, combined with disagreement over the funding of the Centre, eventually put paid to both the relationship and the Centre.

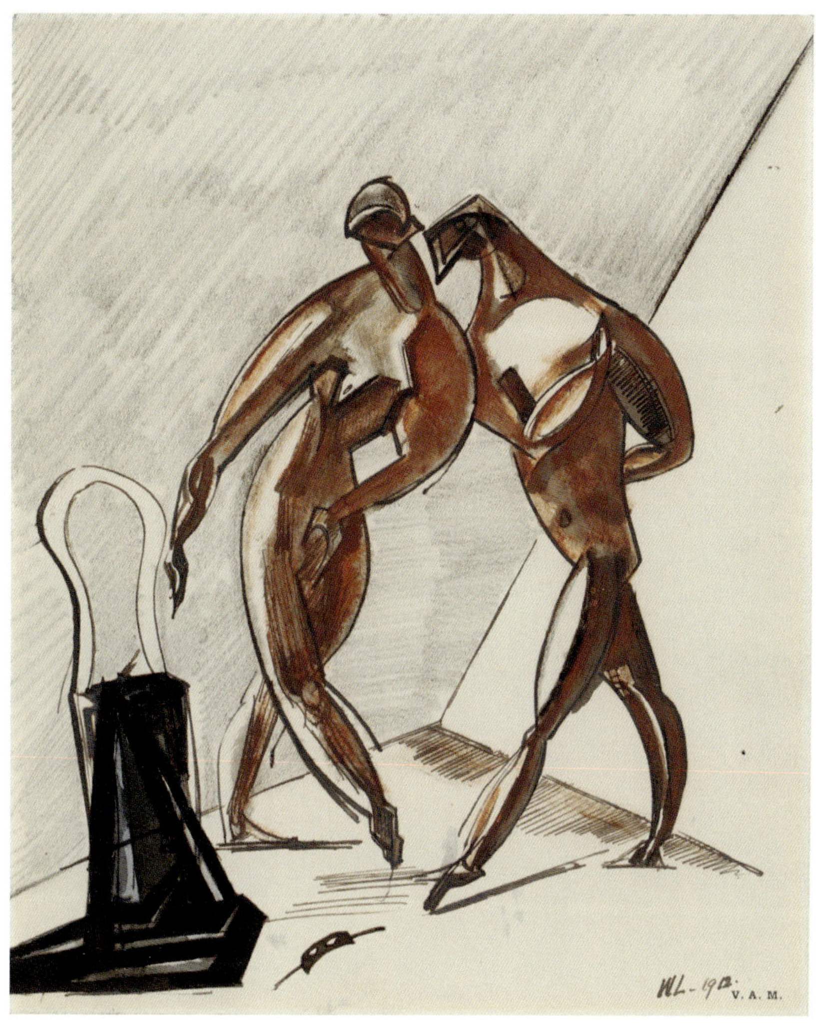

THE DOMINO, 1912
Watercolour, ink and pencil on paper, 25.5 x 20 cm
Victoria and Albert Museum, London: E.3784–1919

In his drawing Lewis applies Cubist rendering of form to a satirical take on the 'primitivism'
of Henri Matisse. It pictures two nude figures (a favourite compositional device of
Lewis's) involved in a balletic ritual courtship whereby one invites the other to don a
mask and cape (or 'domino'). The image expresses Lewis's interest in developing a
narrative dimension to his modernism while also exploring a fascination with disguising
or assuming an identity. That this occurs within the context of the 'masque', the courtly
entertainment of concealed identity, demonstrates Lewis's continued interest in the
artificial world of the stage.

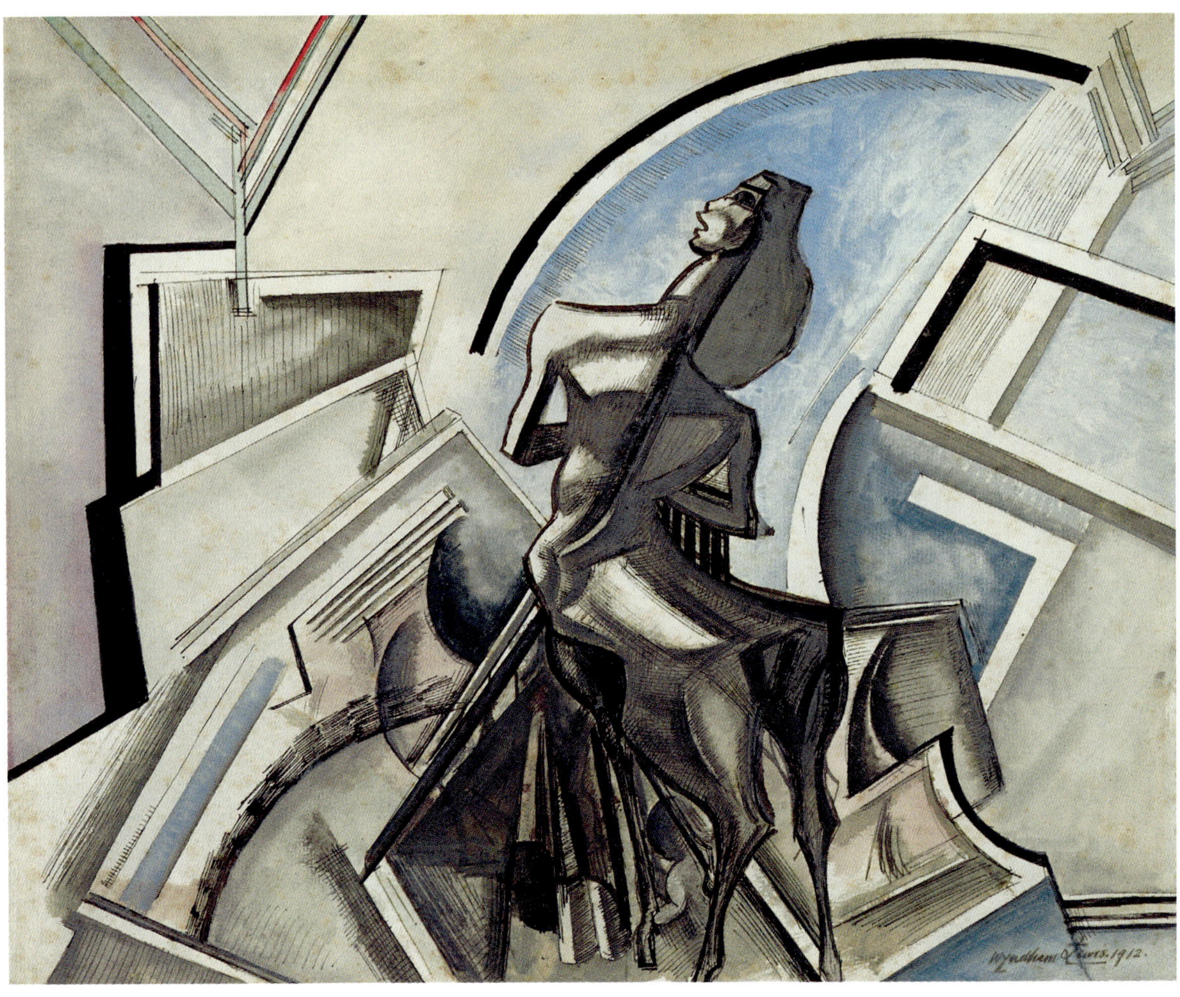

THE CENTAURESS 1, 1912
Pen & ink and wash on paper, 31 x 37 cm
The Higgins Art Gallery and Museum, Bedford: P.138

During 1912 Lewis gradually abandoned his clumsy figure
compositions that parodied the idylls of Matisse and Expressionism,
and instead evolved a new Cubist-influenced visual language, based
on mechanical and architectural forms. This would eventually develop
into the almost pure abstraction of Vorticism in 1914–15.

Lewis's *The Centauress 1* is thus remarkable for the stylistic
transition that seems to occur within the drawing. Its awkwardly
drawn female centaur – a typically ironic Arcadian reference –
appears about to be consumed by an expanding matrix of harsh,
angular forms. Although unwieldy and unresolved, the drawing
nevertheless heralds an era of new aesthetic possibilities for the artist.

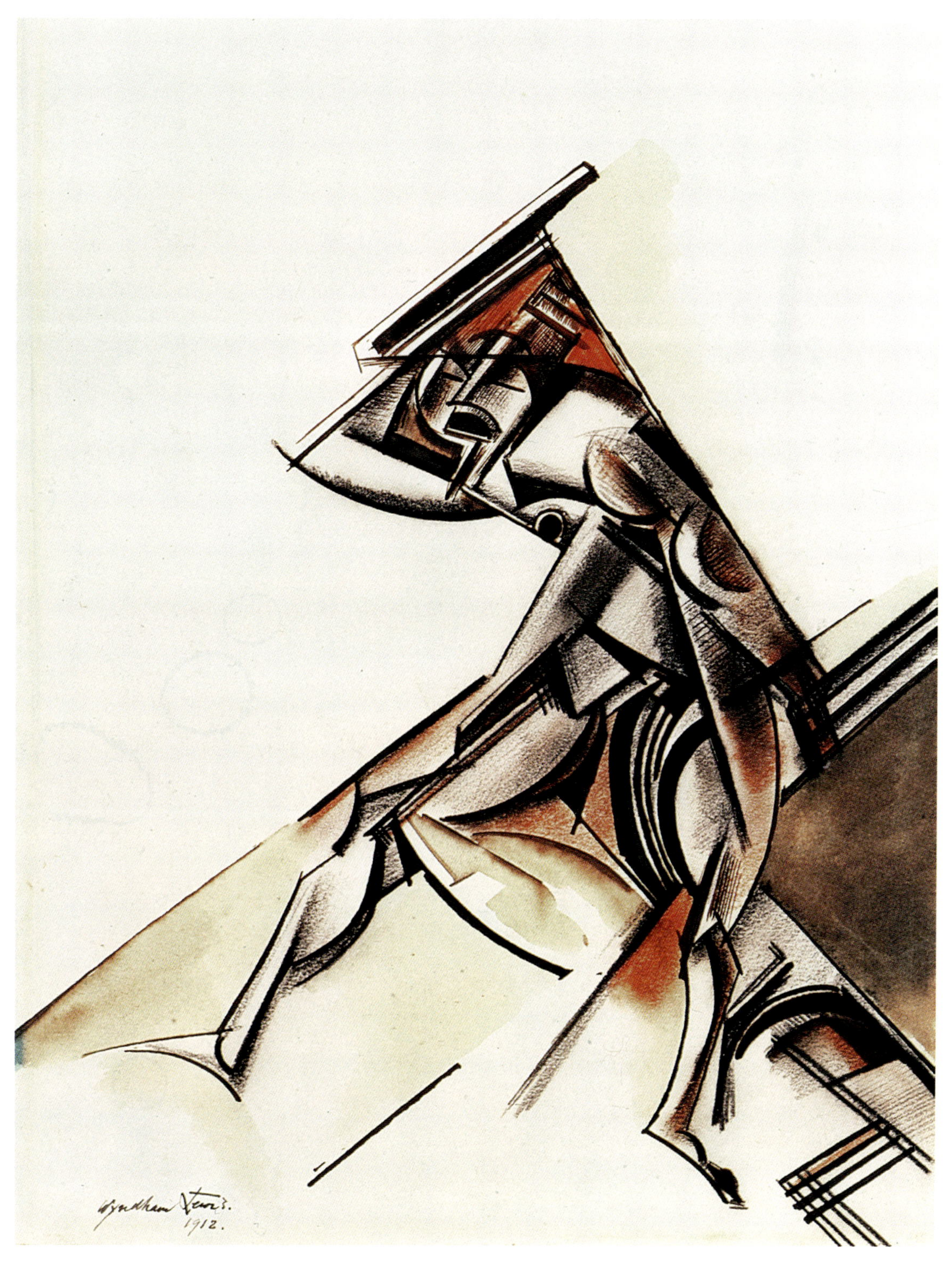

THE VORTICIST, 1912
Ink and watercolour on paper, 41.4 x 29.4 cm
Southampton City Art Gallery, Southampton: 1429

Lewis's drawing *The Vorticist* is an accomplished early engagement with the Cubo-Futurist aesthetic
– the figure's reduction to geometric, mechanical elements anticipates his evolution of Vorticism two
years later. This may account for the drawing's title, probably conferred later by its original owner and
fellow Vorticist, Edward Wadsworth. The figure's apparent anguish shares an affinity with Lewis's *Timon
of Athens* suite of the same period, illustrating the descent of the Shakespearean anti-hero (see p.8).
Both demonstrated a conscious and concerted effort by Lewis to explore the expressive and narrative
potential of the Cubist idiom.

AT THE SEASIDE, 1913
Watercolour, ink and pencil on paper, 47.5 x 31.5 cm
Victoria and Albert Museum, London: E 3763-1919

Lewis's drawing *At the Seaside* marked a return to a more intelligible style after
the Cubist experimentation of *The Vorticist*. Many commentators consider its
incongruous figure grouping, with its bulky male in a bowler hat, to be a sardonic
image of vacationing English bourgeoisie.

Lewis seems also to have had an eye on artistic developments in Europe, the
diverse physiognomies of the figures recalling Pablo Picasso's proto-Cubist *Les
Desmoiselles d'Avignon* (1909). The disparity of size between its protagonists
offers a suggestion too of the melancholic circus performers of the Spanish artist's
Rose Period, though Lewis adds a satirical twist by supplanting them with the
preposterous middle-class. This aspect displeased the Bloomsbury critic, Clive
Bell, who felt Lewis was 'inclined to modify his forms in the interests of drama and
psychology to the detriment of pure design.' Such divergence in artistic opinion
was eventually to descend into personal animosity between these two major
figures in British art.

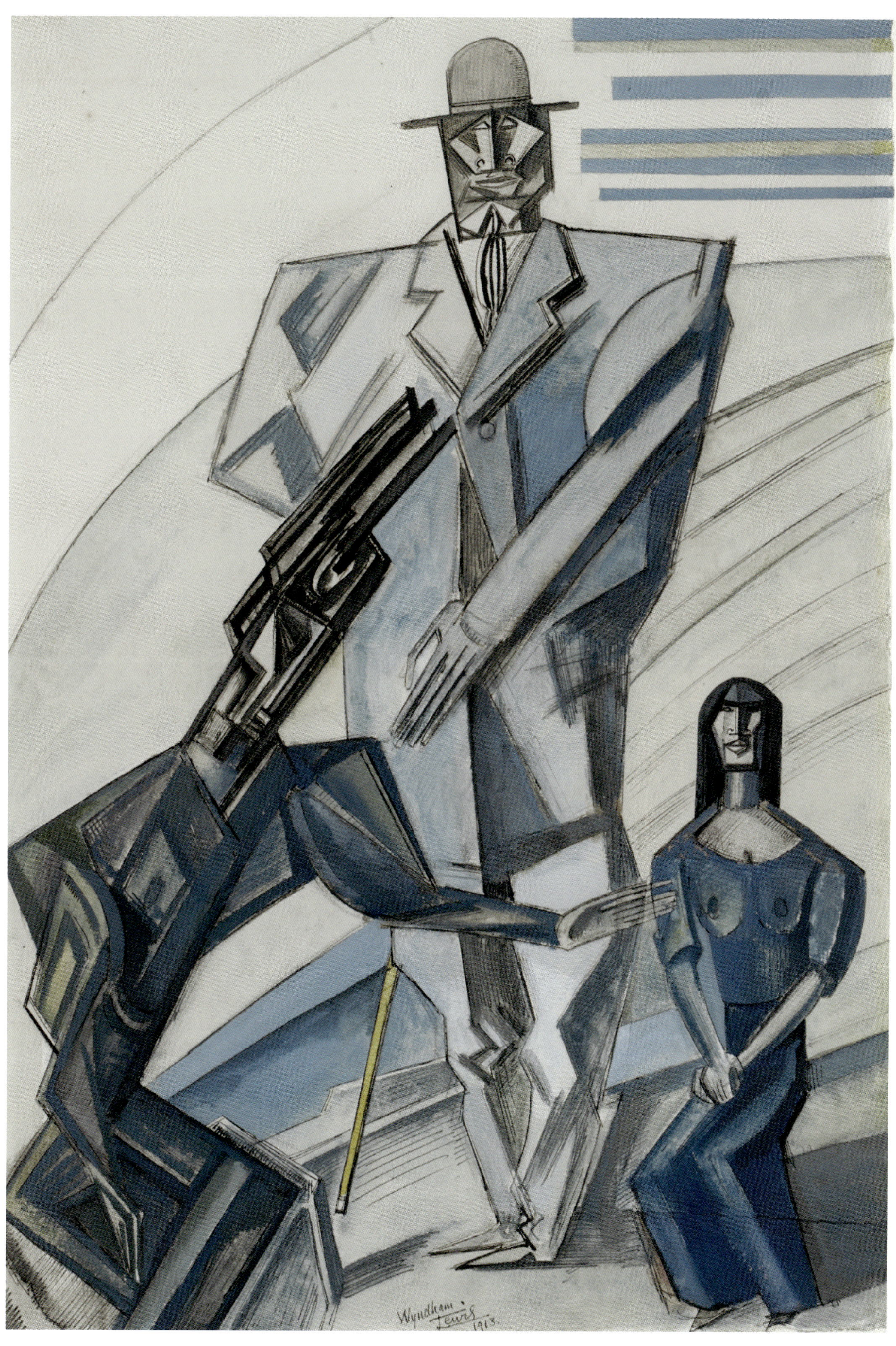

Wyndham Lewis
1913.

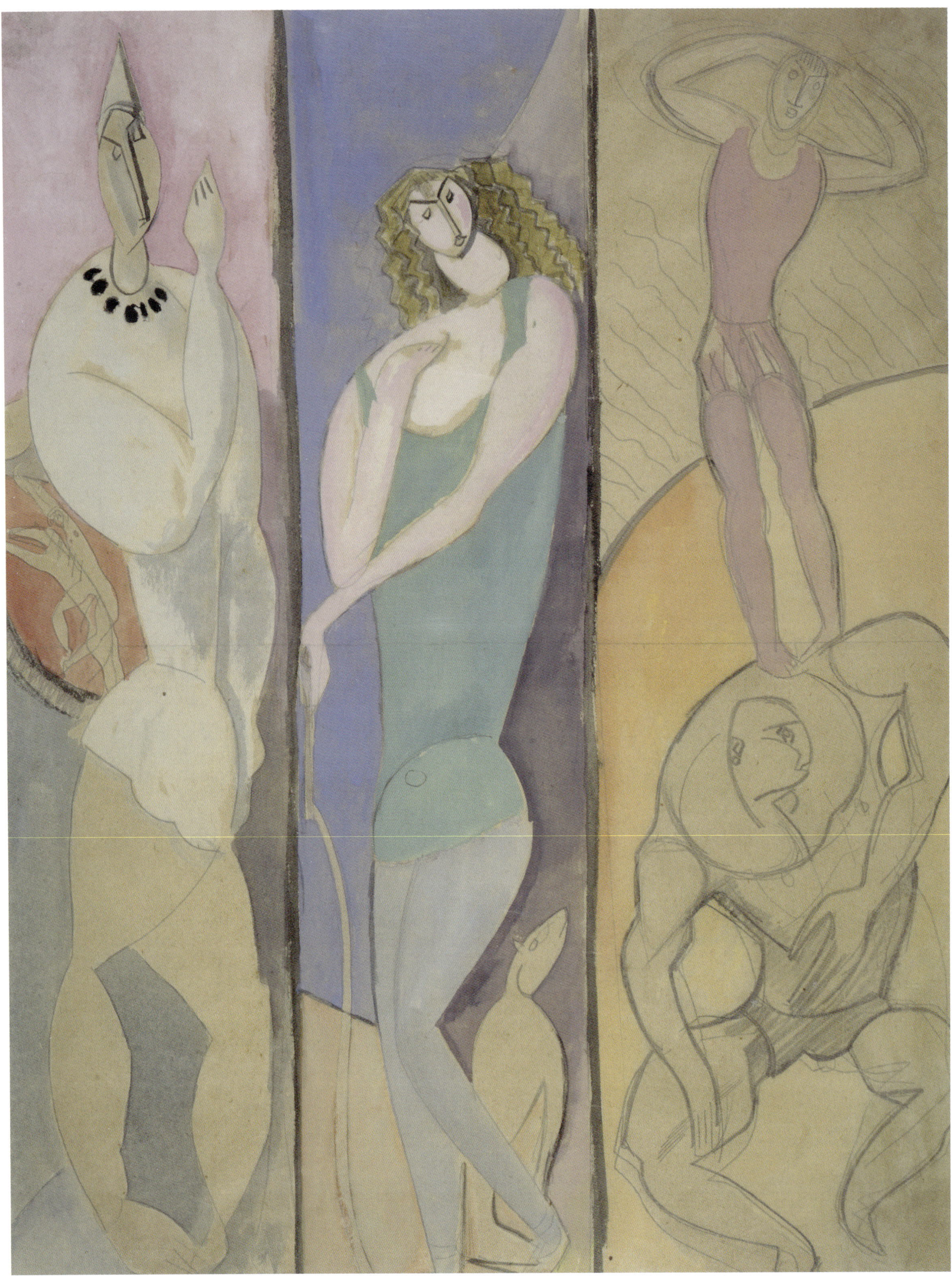

DESIGN FOR A SCREEN, 1913
Pencil and watercolour on paper, 51 x 38.5 cm
Victoria and Albert Museum, London: E.735–1955

In July 1913 Lewis joined the Omega Workshops. The workshops were founded by the critic and artist, Roger Fry, to embed the modern aesthetic within British daily life with a select group of young artists producing a range of textiles and household wares.

For an artist as ambitious as Lewis, submission to the leadership of another and the anonymity of a collective may have seemed unusual. This would underestimate Fry's influence over British art in the early twentieth century, founded mainly on his two ground-breaking Post-Impressionist exhibitions in 1910 and 1912. These introduced to the British public the art of van Gogh, Matisse, Picasso and Cézanne, as well as work by British *avant-garde* artists, including Lewis.

To the relatively unknown Lewis, closer association with Fry and his powerful Bloomsbury friends must have seemed prudent. However, relations quickly soured between Fry and Lewis at the Omega Workshops, culminating in a bitter public feud over ownership of a contract to decorate the *Daily Mail*'s Ideal Home Exhibition. The dispute provided Lewis with the impetus to leave Omega, but not before he created this design for a screen. In it he foregoes previous Cubist experiments and applies a decorative figuration more attuned to Bloomsbury taste. His incorporation of circus performers reflected a vogue originating in the art of Henri de Toulouse-Lautrec and Pablo Picasso's melancholic 'Saltimbanque' images.

RED DUET, 1914
Chalk and gouache on paper, 38.5 x 56 cm
Ivor Braka Ltd, London

Lewis described Vorticism as 'dogmatically anti-real', and its 'ultimate aim was to exclude from painting the everyday visual real altogether'. *Red Duet* serves these principles by transposing Futurism's fragmented mechanical and architectural forms to create dissonant image of gyrating shapes and angles.

Although the drawing affirms Lewis's belief that the 'world of machinery' was as real as natural forms, and so legitimate inspiration for art, it resists the Futurist's romantic devotion to mechanisation. Instead, as the title suggests, the drawing visualises a corresponding, or conflicting, 'dualism' which Lewis saw as a fundamental prerequisite of creativity. This was reflected in his apparently contradictory opening statement in his edict 'Vortex No.1', appearing in *BLAST No.2* in 1915: 'You must talk with two tongues, if you do not wish to cause confusion.'

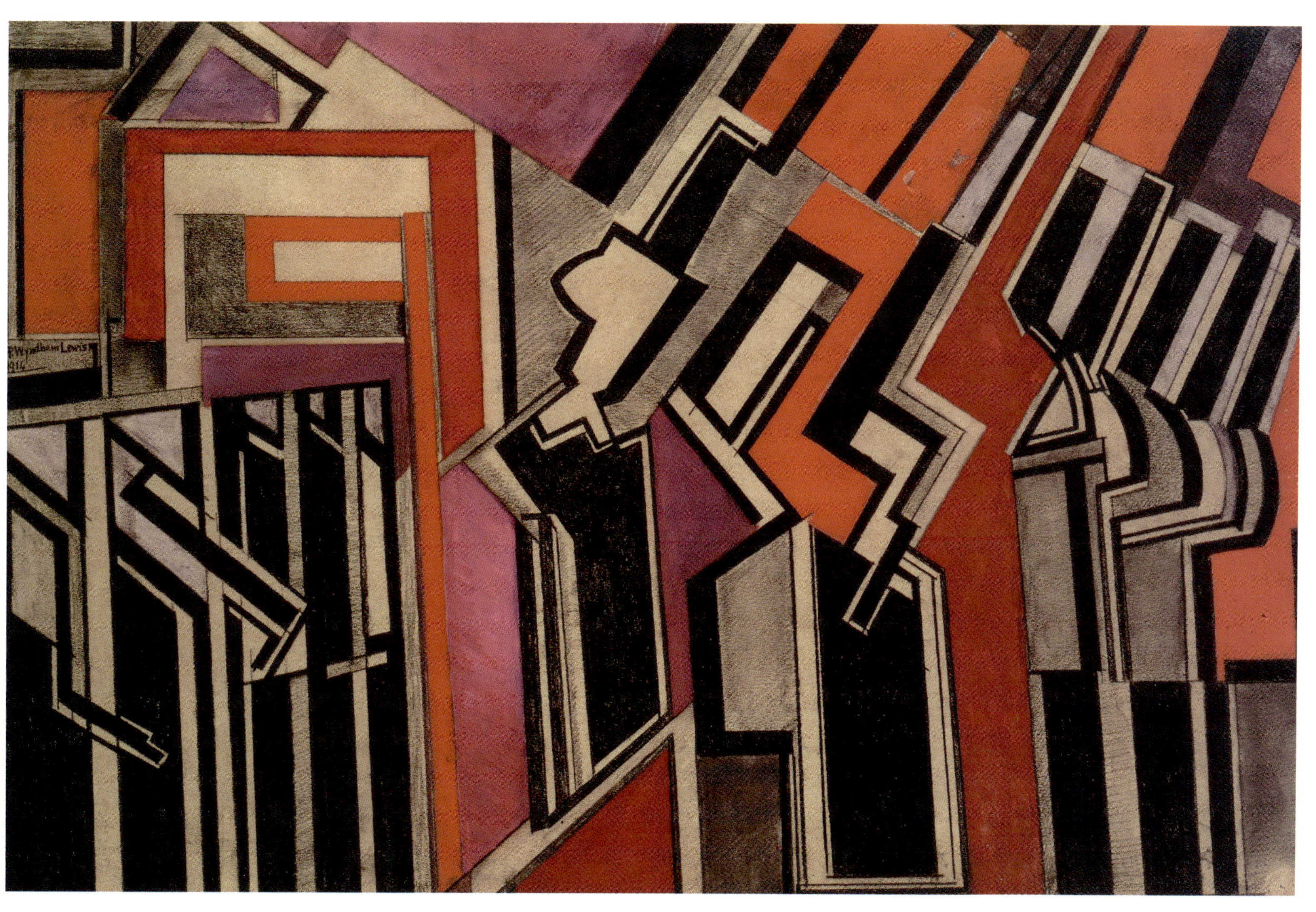

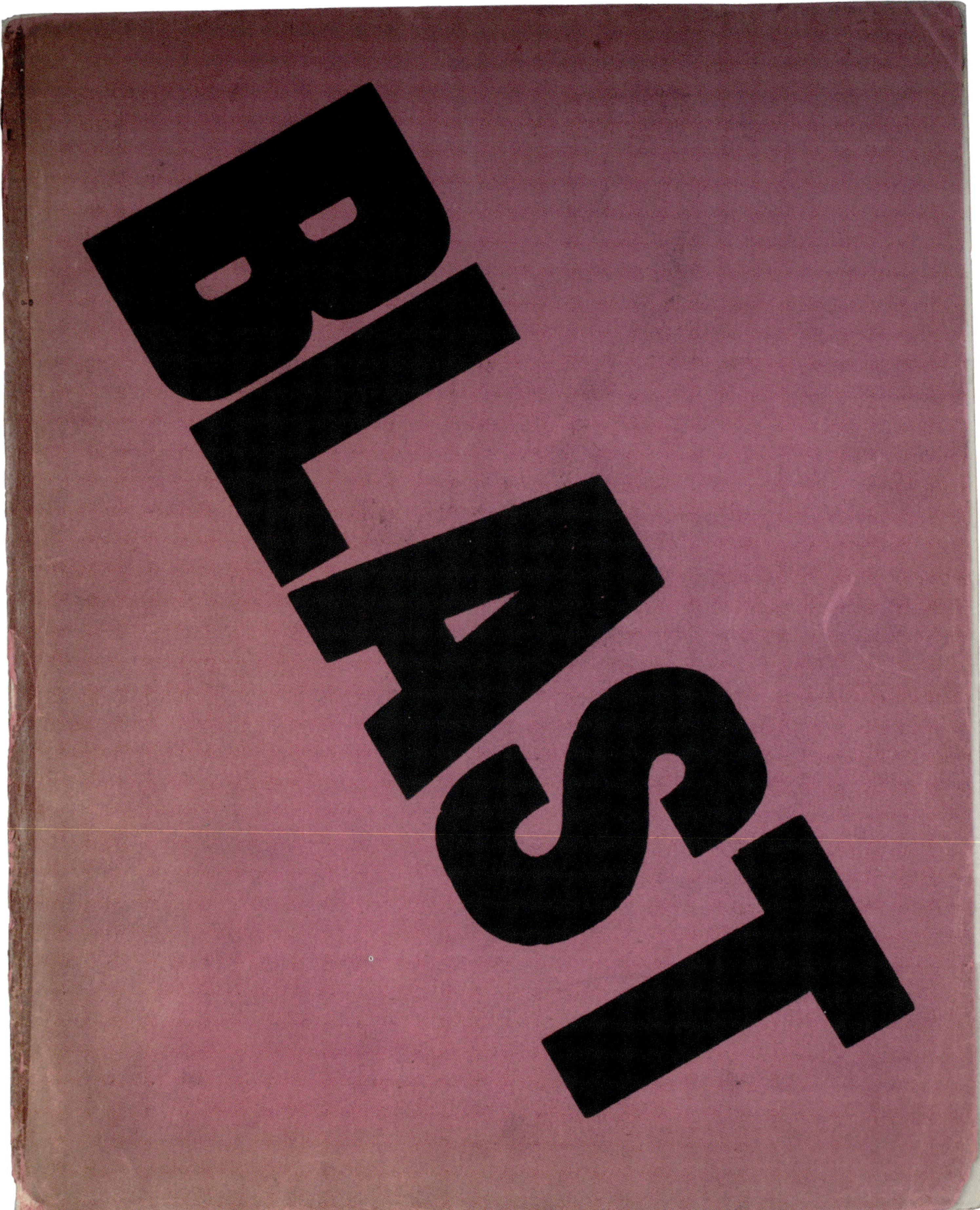
BLAST

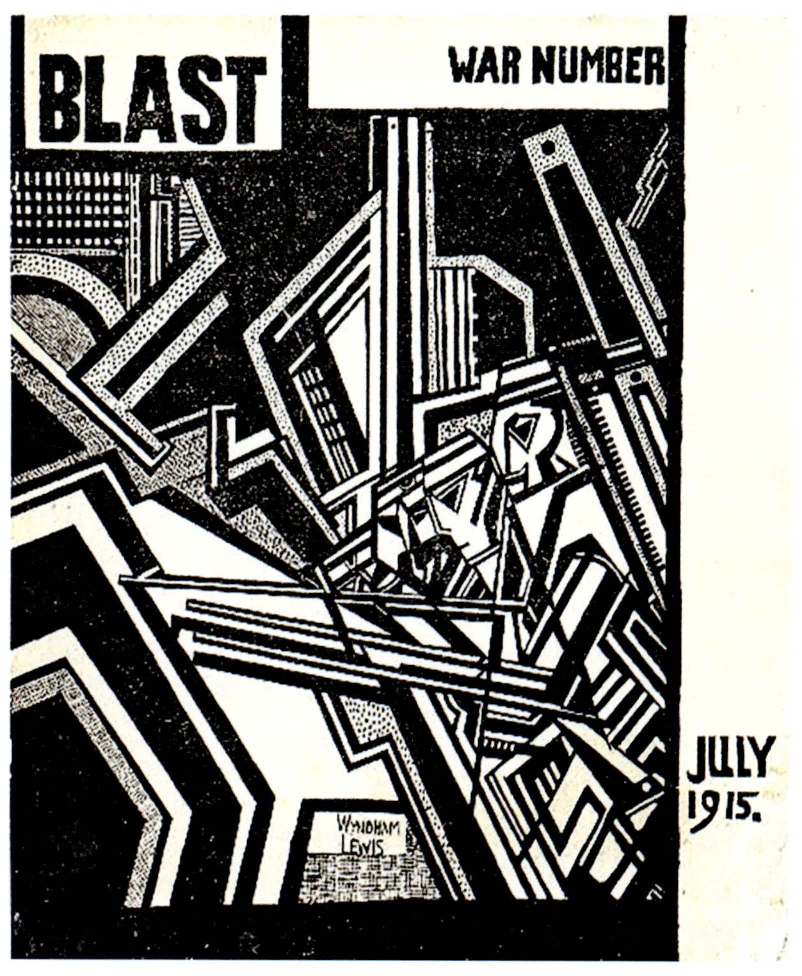

BLAST 1, 1914
UCL Art Museum, London: 4638

BLAST 2: WAR NUMBER, 1915
IWM: LBY 83/4137

On 2 July 1914 Lewis launched *BLAST*, so announcing the arrival of Vorticism. Part polemic, part manifesto, part absurdist satire, it was undoubtedly one of the great modernist texts of the early twentieth century and a major British contribution to the European *avant-garde*. From its provocative, proto-Punk pink cover, praise of Britain's industry and naval power, and mockery of its petty manners and artistic sensibilities, to the inclusion of Lewis's discordant play, *The Enemy of the Stars, BLAST* embodied the restless iconoclasm of a younger generation on the eve of war.

One year into the First World War, Lewis published a second *BLAST* edition. Subtitled as the 'War Number' and reproducing a monochrome woodcut by Lewis on the cover, it lacked the visual impact of its predecessor. Much of the content was Lewis's, but it notably included two poems, *Preludes* and *Rhapsody on a Windy Night,* by T S Eliot, whom Lewis had met and befriended several months earlier. Its visual content was typically war themed, with abstract and semi-abstract images reproduced bearing titles like *Combat* and *War Engine.* Poignantly, it contained a death notice for the sculptor and Vorticist signatory, Henri Gaudier-Brezska, killed in action a month earlier.

In March 1916, Lewis enlisted with the Royal Garrison Artillery, ending any prospect of a further edition and also spelling the demise of Vorticism as an artistic force.

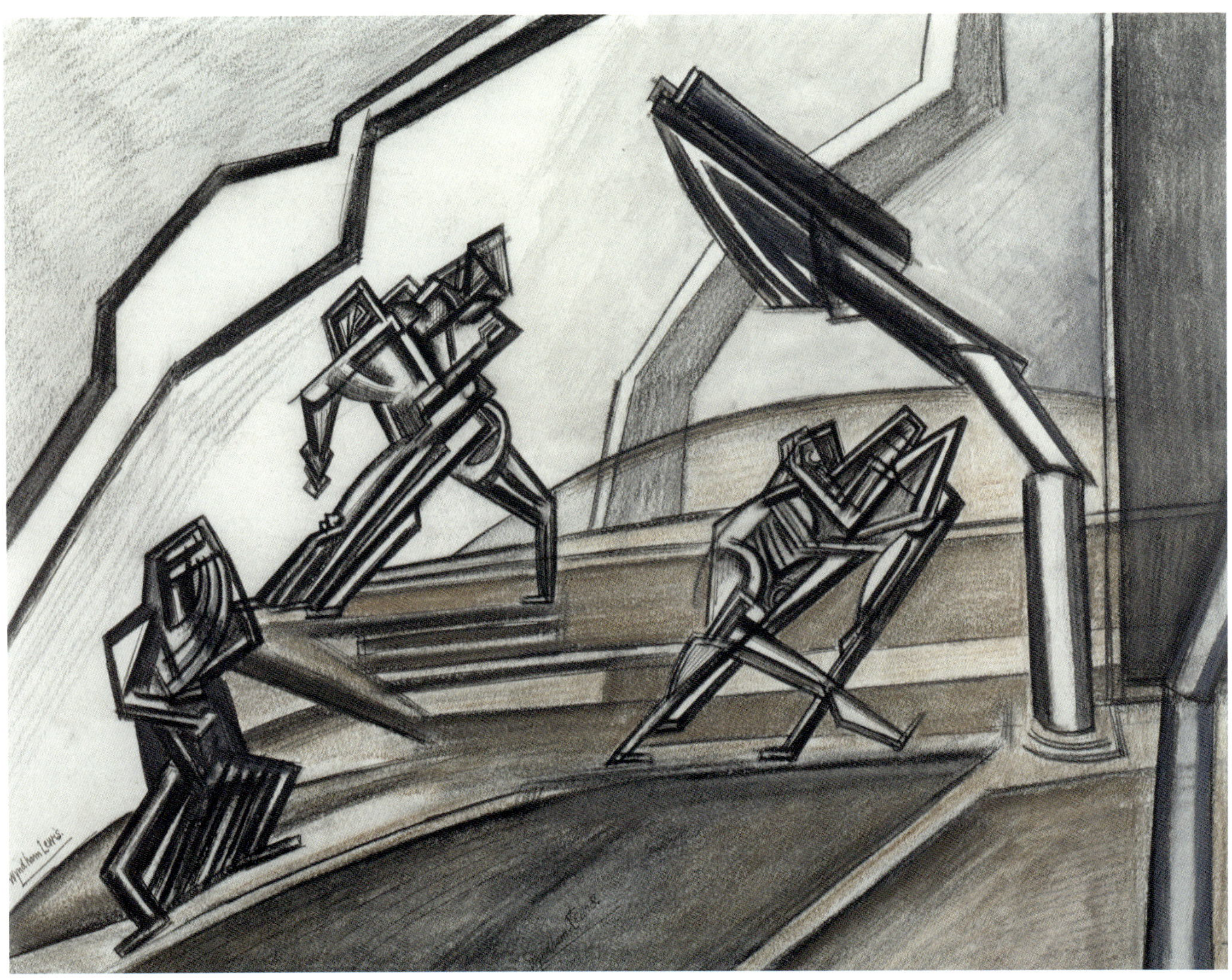

COMBAT NO.2, 1914
Pastel and ink, 27.6 x 33.3 cm
Victoria and Albert Museum, London: E.3760–1919

Set in barren landscape, mechanical humanoids wrestle to attain primitive masculine dominance. Their prize is a female, in dress-like garb, standing left awaiting the attentions of the victorious suitor. Created in 1914, shortly before the outbreak of the First World War, *Combat No.2* appears to serve as a metaphor for the aggressive stand-off between major European powers seeking ascendancy over continental rivals. It bears also a dispiriting summation of the influential theories of Henri Bergson, suggesting that humanity's unreasoned embrace of a universal life-force merely results in debased, animalistic behaviour.

THE CROWD, 1914–15
Oil on canvas, 200.7 x 153.7 cm
Tate: T00689

With its interlocking architectural planes and cascading abstract forms, *The Crowd* was Vorticism's standout painting. First exhibited at the Second London Group exhibition in March 1915, this schematic cityscape is often paired with *The Crowd Master*, Lewis's account of the behaviour of London crowds in the days building up to the First World War. However, discernible figures bearing flags suggest not a war-fevered crowd but an insurrectionist throng. This is supported by the painting's alternative title of *Revolution*.

Whatever its nature, *The Crowd* illustrates Lewis's interest in the emerging science of 'crowd psychology'. The assertion by its chief exponent, the French author Gustave le Bon, that the individual 'is no longer himself ... but has become an automaton who has ceased to be guided by his will' is visualised by Lewis in the tumbling, irregular mass that breaks and reforms as it negotiates the rigid planes and grids of the built environment. *The Crowd* also reveals Lewis's waking interest in popular movements and power relations, a curiosity that would eventually have disastrous consequences for him.

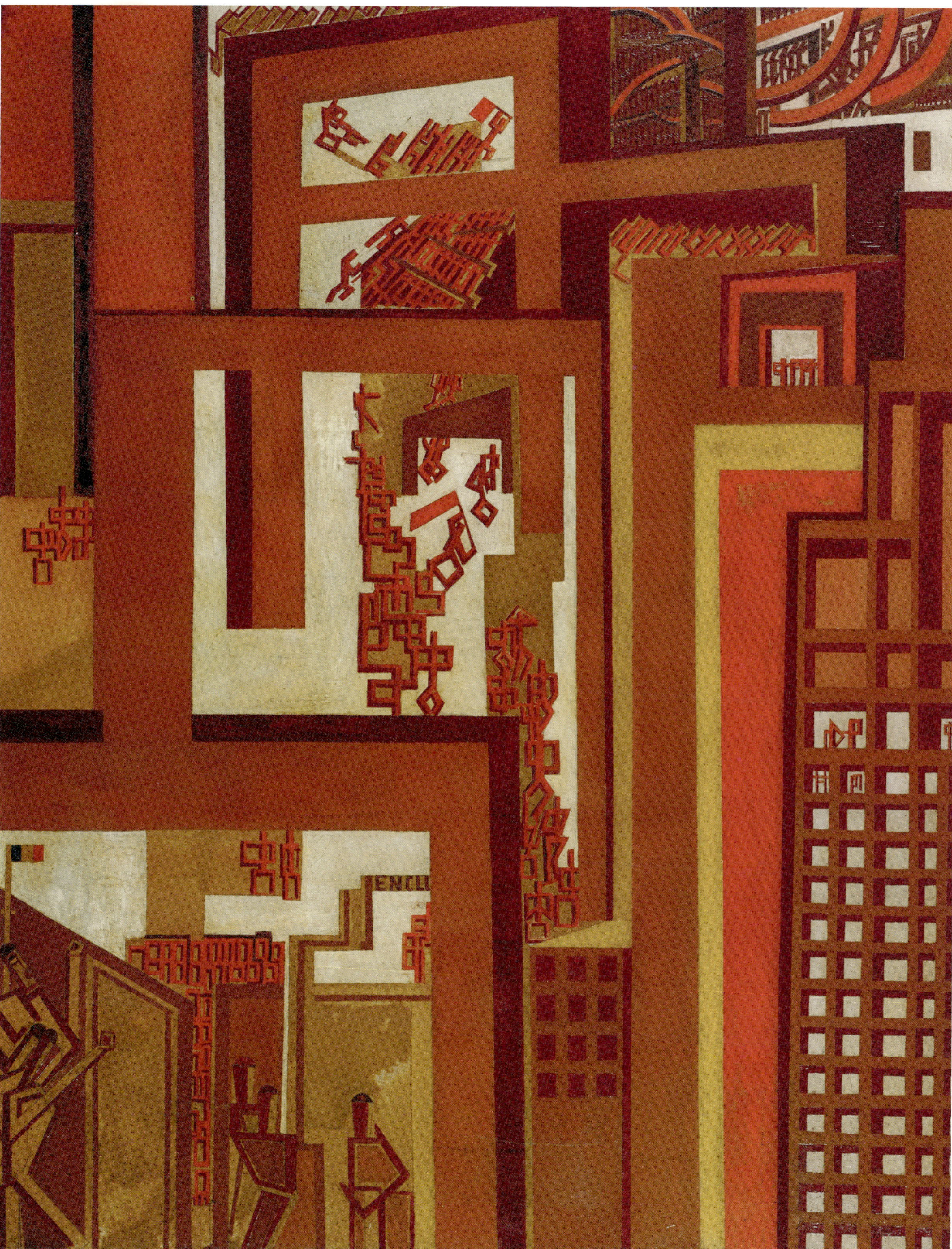
ENCL

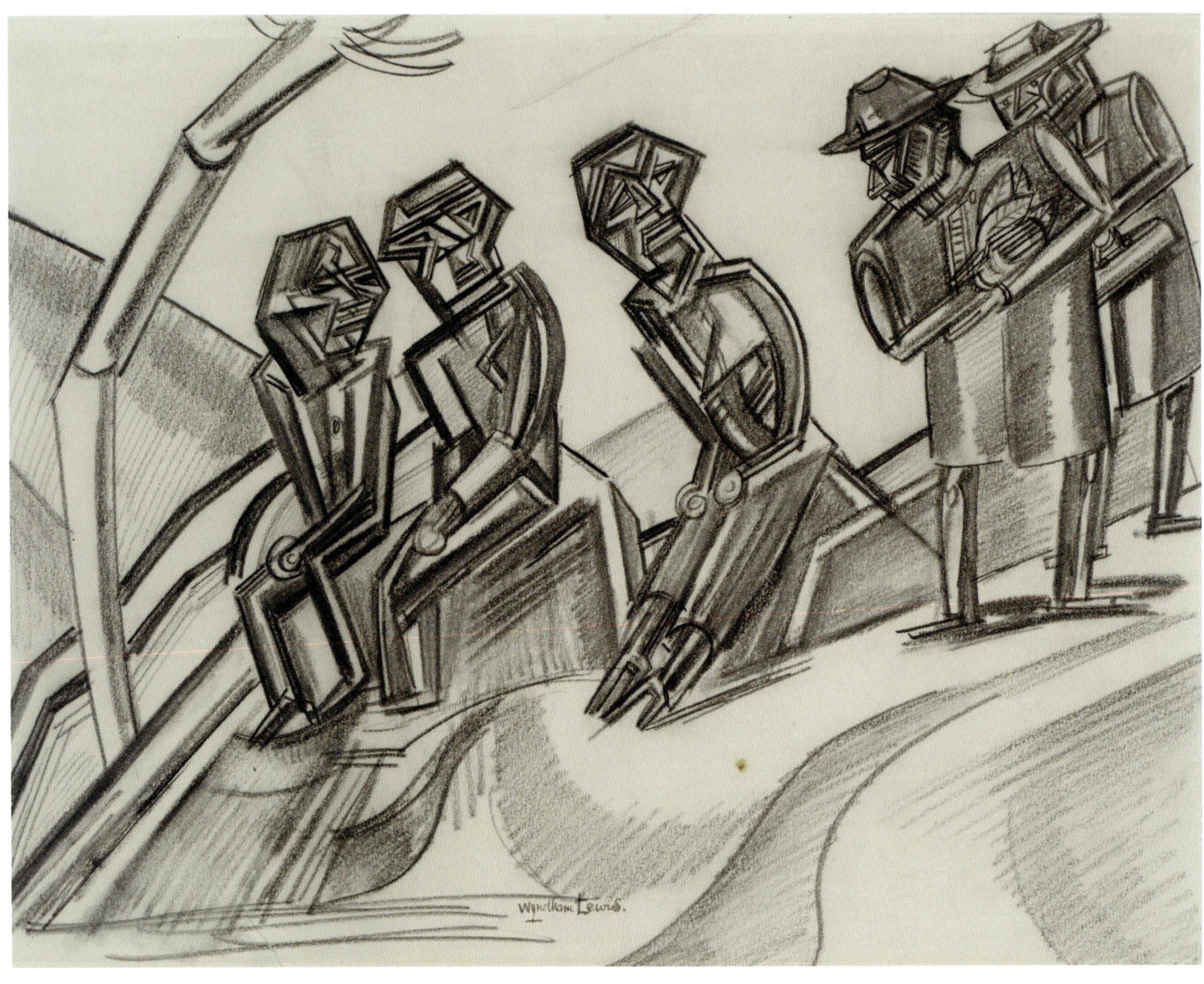

TWO MISSIONARIES, 1917
Black crayon on paper, 30.5 x 35 cm
Victoria and Albert Museum, London: E.3771–1919

Lewis's service as a subaltern with the Royal Garrison Artillery during the First World War caused a brief hiatus in his art. This ended in June 1917 when he executed a number of drawings while recovering from 'trench fever' in Dieppe. These made little reference to the ongoing war, tending instead to reflect his surroundings and in particular the Post-Impressionist associations with the northern French coastline. Stylistically, he re-engaged with the geometric figuration of his pre-Vorticist period, resurrecting its satirical element in the process.

Two Missionaries, though an outwardly curious subject, satirises the primitivism of Paul Gauguin and other Post-Impressionists. In the 1890s Gauguin, having lived among peasant communities of Brittany, headed to the South Seas in search of ever more primitive idylls. Lewis's drawing mocks such aspirations showing three Cubist indigenes, whose tropical innocence is about to be undermined by two European missionaries.

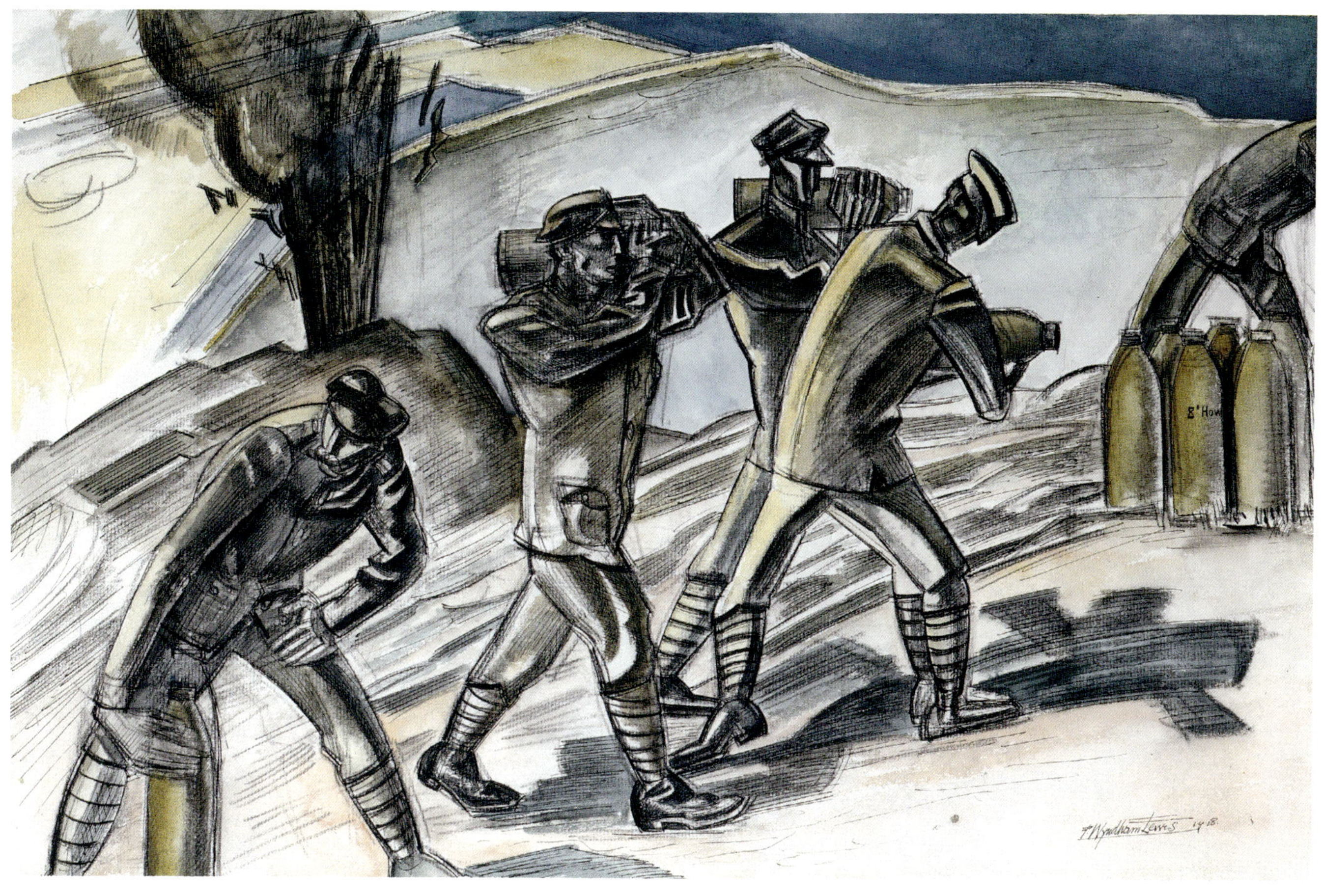

SHELL-HUMPING (or HOWITZERS), 1918
Ink, chalk and watercolour on paper, 31.5 x 47.3 cm
Norfolk Museums Service (Norwich Castle Museum and Art Gallery)

In December 1917 Lewis was commissioned as a Canadian official war artist. Coinciding with this
appointment, he began a series of independently produced drawings that served as a visual memoir
of his time on the Western Front. *Shell-Humping* typifies the stylised figuration employed in the series,
described by Lewis as 'a direct, ready formula to give interpretation to what I took part in, in France'.
This approach arose from Lewis's belief that no meaningful or lasting expression of the war in art was
possible while it was still in progress – 'truth has no place in action', he would claim.

   Shell-Humping thus provides a readable image of British artillerymen involved in the gruelling work
of moving 100-lbs shells for firing by the standard British 6-inch howitzer. This lies off picture, enabling
focus on the men serving it and the wider war machine. Their geometric, robotic appearance attest
to the de-personalising nature of army routine and discipline, though the human exhaustion each
exhibits makes their subservience appear more disturbing.

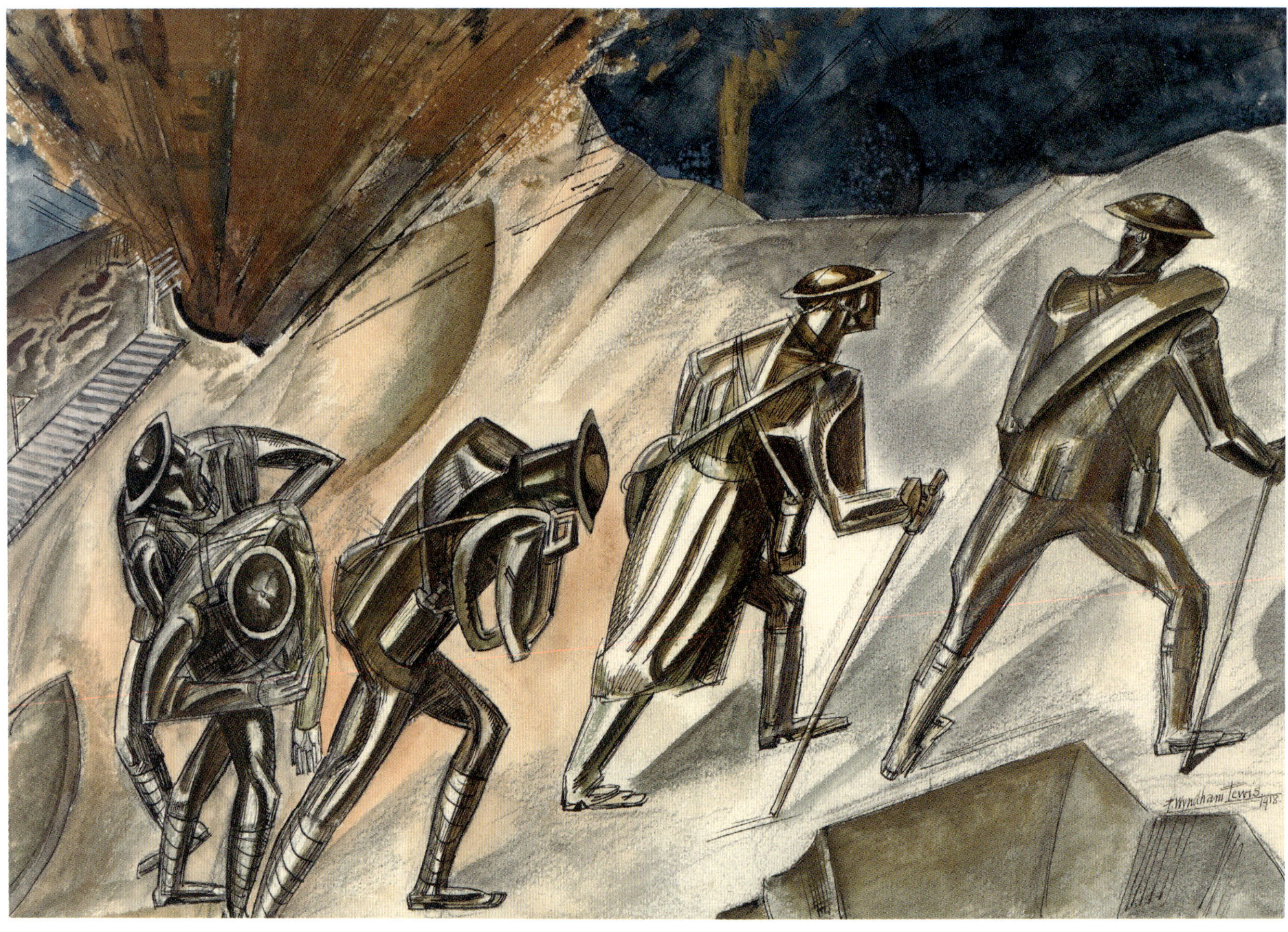

OFFICER AND SIGNALLERS, 1918
Ink, watercolour and gouache on paper, 33.8 x 44.2 cm
IWM: IWM ART 5932

During the First World War, Lewis served with the Royal Garrison Artillery until he was commissioned
as a war artist by the Canadians in December 1917. Alongside this, Lewis embarked on a series
of drawings as a visual memoir of his time on the Western Front. One such drawing, *Officer and
Signallers*, presents an image of contrasts, from the cool inky blue of the night sky to the warm
earth hues of the shell-burst on the left. This highlights the drawing's central theme – the opposing
relationship between an animalistic instinct for survival and machine-like adherence to military duty,
which Lewis saw as a key aspect of life at the front. This is captured in the rear signallers, who cower
before the explosion, and the leading soldiers who march mechanically on regardless.

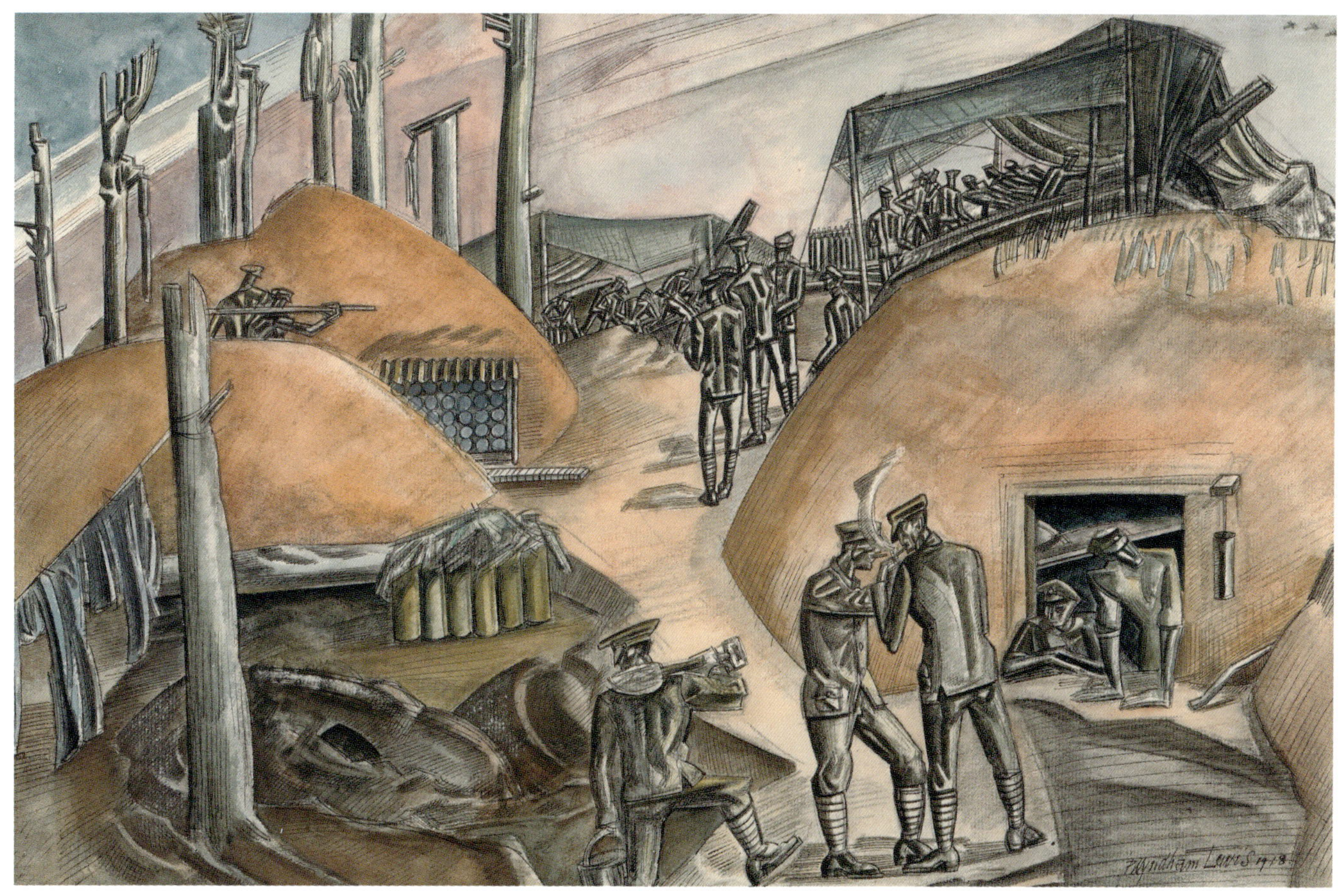

BATTERY POSITION IN A WOOD, 1918
Ink, crayon, watercolour, 43.8 x 58.4 cm
IWM: IWM ART 1672

Battery Position in a Wood forms part of the same visual wartime memoir as *Shell-Humping* (p.39) and *Officer and Signallers* (opposite). The drawing shows Lewis's artillerymen now in a period of inactivity, idly conversing and smoking together. The implicit message is one of restored humanity amid a hiatus from military duty and discipline. The washing line strung from a tree stump adds a further disarming note of domesticity.

A BATTERY SHELLED, 1919
Oil on canvas, 182.8 x 317.5 cm
IWM: IWM ART 2747

Having been appointed as a Canadian official war
artist, Lewis was simultaneously employed by the
British in 1918 under their British War Memorial
Committee scheme. Under this Lewis created his
most important war painting, *A Battery Shelled*.

Showing the German shelling of a British
artillery battery, *A Battery Shelled* distilled Lewis's
thoughts on the effect of modern warfare. His
gunners appear dehumanised and insect-like,
scuttling for cover, governed by primitive instincts
for survival in much the manner of the beings in
Lewis's earlier *Combat No.2* drawing (p.36). Lewis
likened the First World War to an absurd nightmare,
removed from everyday reality. This sense of surreal
spectacle is articulated in the painting by the three
large foreground artillerymen, whose naturalistic
appearance heightens their disengagement and
apparent disbelief or indifference to the chaos
before them.

Although this painting was the only major
British modernist canvas to emerge from the First
World War, it did not restore Lewis's leadership of
the British *avant-garde*. Shown alongside other
memorial canvases at the Royal Academy in 1919,
it provoked hostility in the press and Parliament.
Shaken by the reaction, its owners, the Imperial War
Museum, loaned it long-term to the Tate Gallery
shortly afterwards.

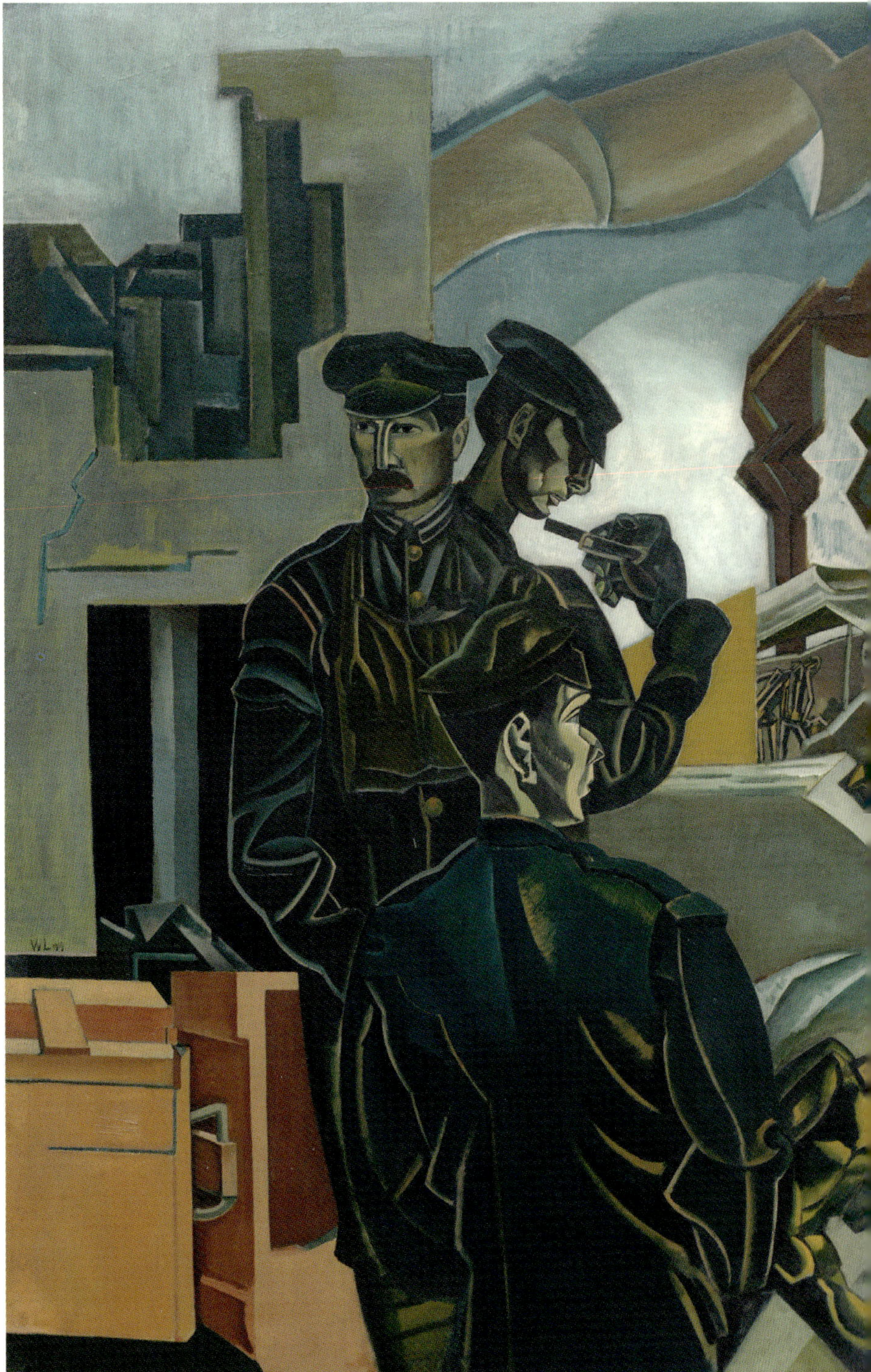

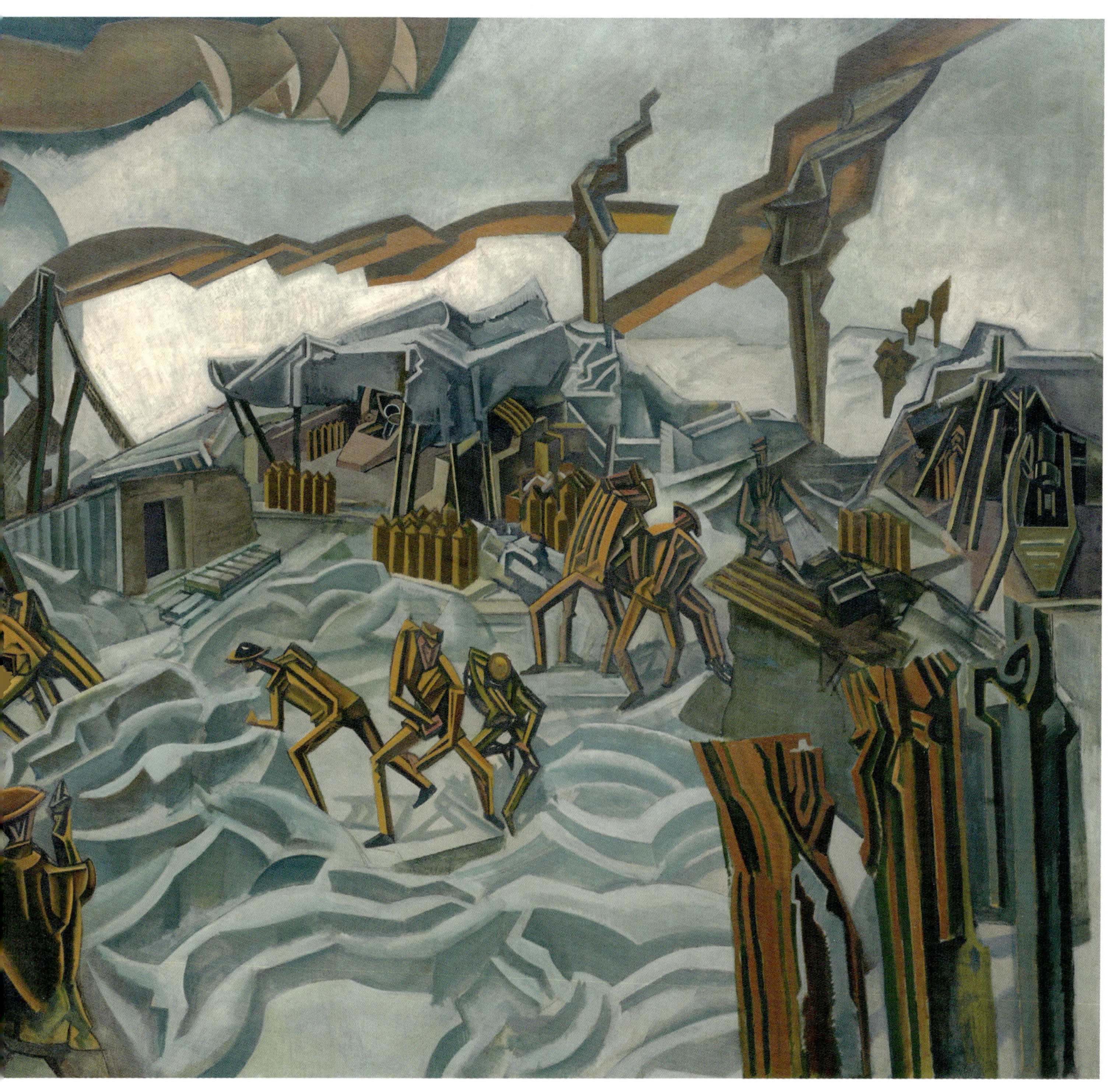

A READING OF OVID (TYROS), 1920–21
Oil on canvas, 165.2 x 90.2 cm
Scottish National Gallery of Modern Art

The inter-war period is often regarded as a time when Lewis created little art, preferring instead to concentrate on writing. However, he continued to experiment artistically, especially in the early 1920s and most obviously with his invention of the 'tyro'. For Lewis tyros were imaginary beings that embodied the listlessness and uncertainty pervading British society after the First World War. Merging elements of Cubism with African and Oceanic fetish masks, Lewis created a series of grotesquely caricatured images, with which he sought to broaden the scope of modern British art by introducing a satirical note in the manner of William Hogarth (1697–1764) or Thomas Rowlandson (1756–1827).

The chief target of Lewis's satire was the intellectual and artistic affectations of Bloomsbury. *A Reading of Ovid (Tyros)* thus presents two grinning tyros reading a 'classical' author. To emphasise their pretentious studiousness, Lewis has the right-hand figure glance at the viewer to draw attention. The painting's sentiment converged with that of Lewis's short-lived review, *The Tyro*, in which he continued his attack on the Francophile tendencies of Roger Fry and Bloomsbury. Much of Lewis's ire had arisen from a thwarted ambition to establish an internationally recognised British *avant-garde*. War service put paid to this, and he inevitably ceded ground to the pacifists of Bloomsbury.

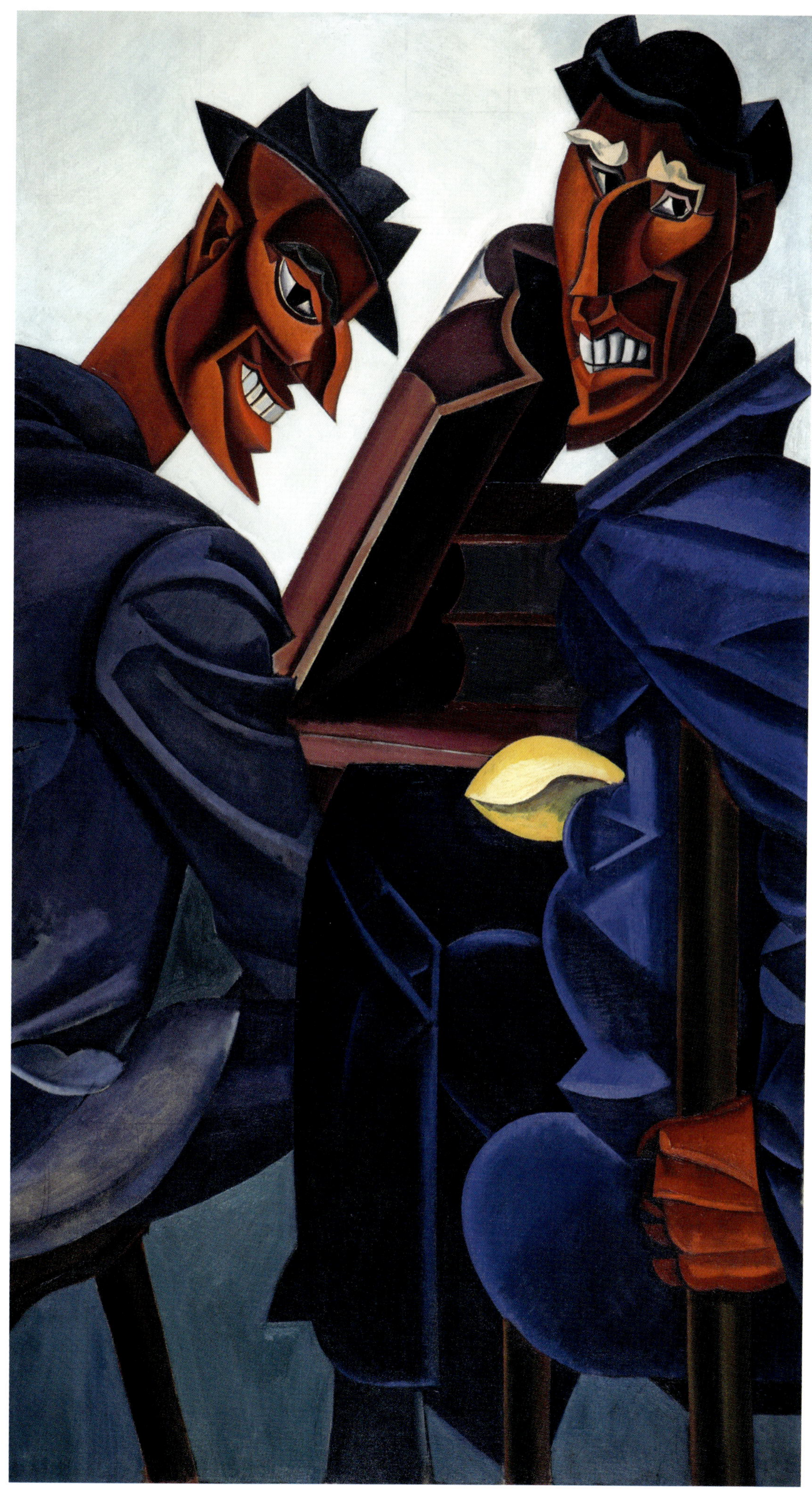

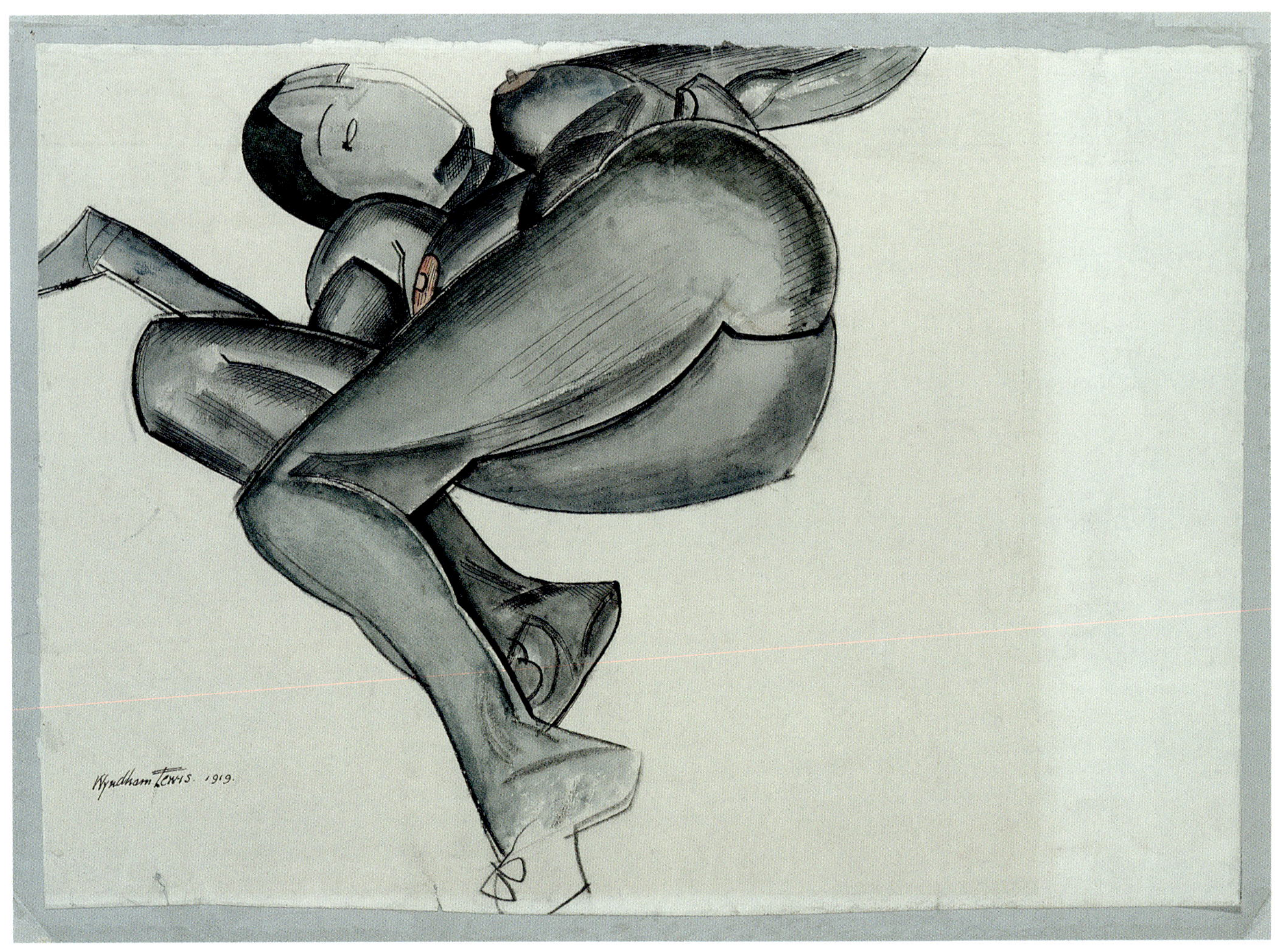

NUDE 1, 1919

Ink and watercolour on paper, 24 x 34 cm
Leeds Art Gallery: LEEAG.1935.0014.0002

In 1919, dissatisfied with his wartime drawings, Lewis attempted to re-fashion his technique, developing a new, linear style. As part of this, Lewis undertook a series of nude studies. *Nude 1* is the most adventurous of these, its bold foreshortening demonstrating Lewis's command of line and innate gift for draughtsmanship. The drawing typically references current Continental styles, notably the slick lines of Art Deco. In doing so, Lewis affirmed his position as a 'classicist', suppressing the humanity of his subject and concerning himself instead with a dispassionate reading of external surfaces and abstract form.

EZRA POUND, 1920
Pencil on paper, 36.1 x 27 cm
National Portrait Gallery: 6728

POET SEATED: EZRA POUND, 1921
Pencil on paper, 38 x 50.6 cm
Manchester Art Gallery: 1925.507

Lewis was introduced to the American poet,
Ezra Pound, by Laurence Binyon in 1909.
Although both men were initially suspicious
of each other, their shared drive and
ambition drew them irresistibly close. Pound
subsequently became Lewis's most important
friend and collaborator, co-founding Vorticism
and providing moral support for Lewis during
his war service. After the war, as Lewis was
reinventing his drawing technique, Pound
frequently sat for him, as these two studies
show.

Ezra Pound exemplified Lewis's new
approach — a vigorous linear figuration,
retaining emphasis on abstract form. This is
most obvious in the solid asymmetrical mass
that forms the poet's generous head of hair.
The influence of Continental contemporaries,
such as Picasso and Modigliani, is clearly
evident, not least their concern for a post-war
art that combined the modernist sensibility
with a reassuringly solid classical formalism. In
Poet Seated, Lewis renders Pound's face mask-
like and expressionless, reflecting the vogue
for African and Oceanic art. This, though, is
countered by the dynamic, sweeping contours
with which Lewis constitutes the seated poet.
Crossed-legged and lapels clasped, Pound
appears as a study of barely contained energy.

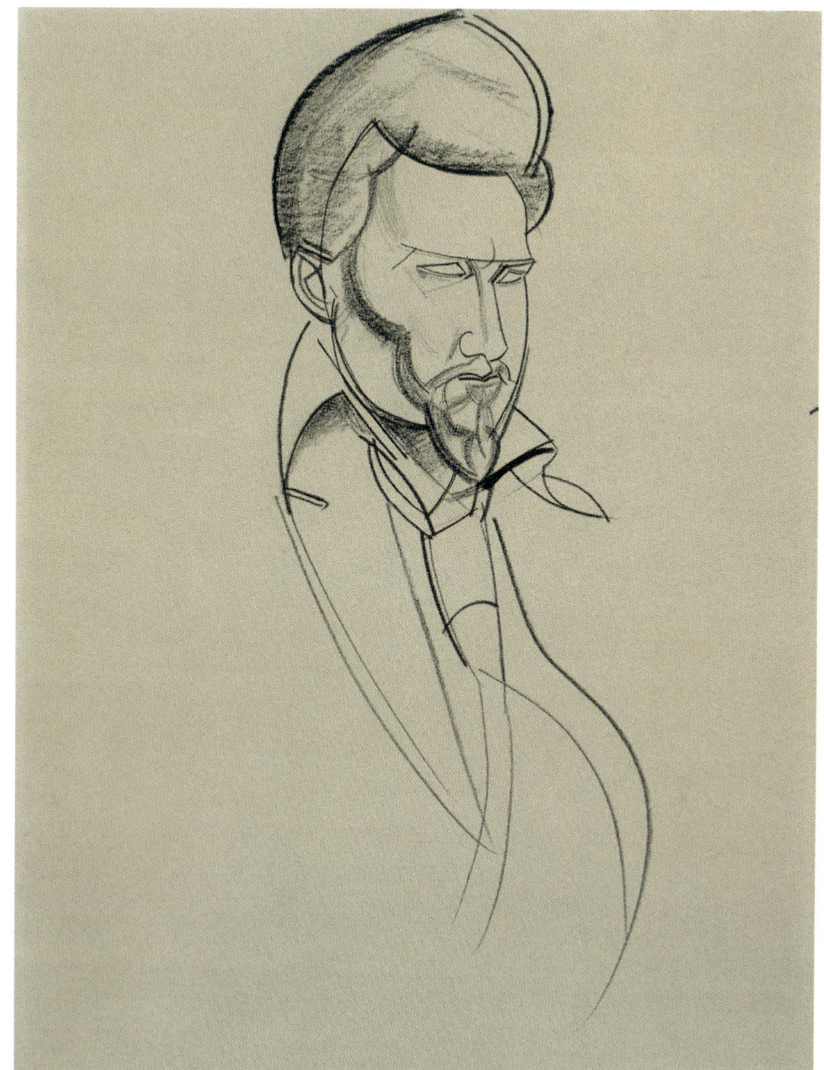

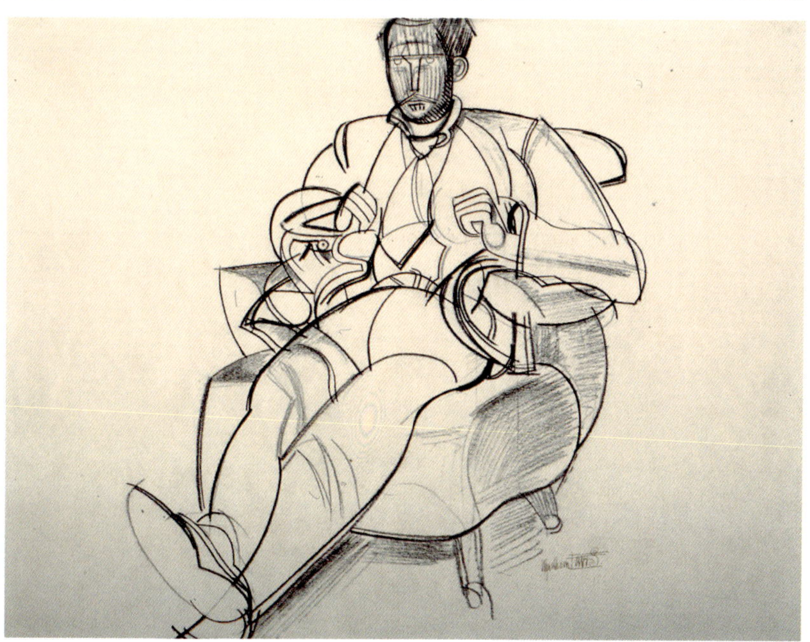

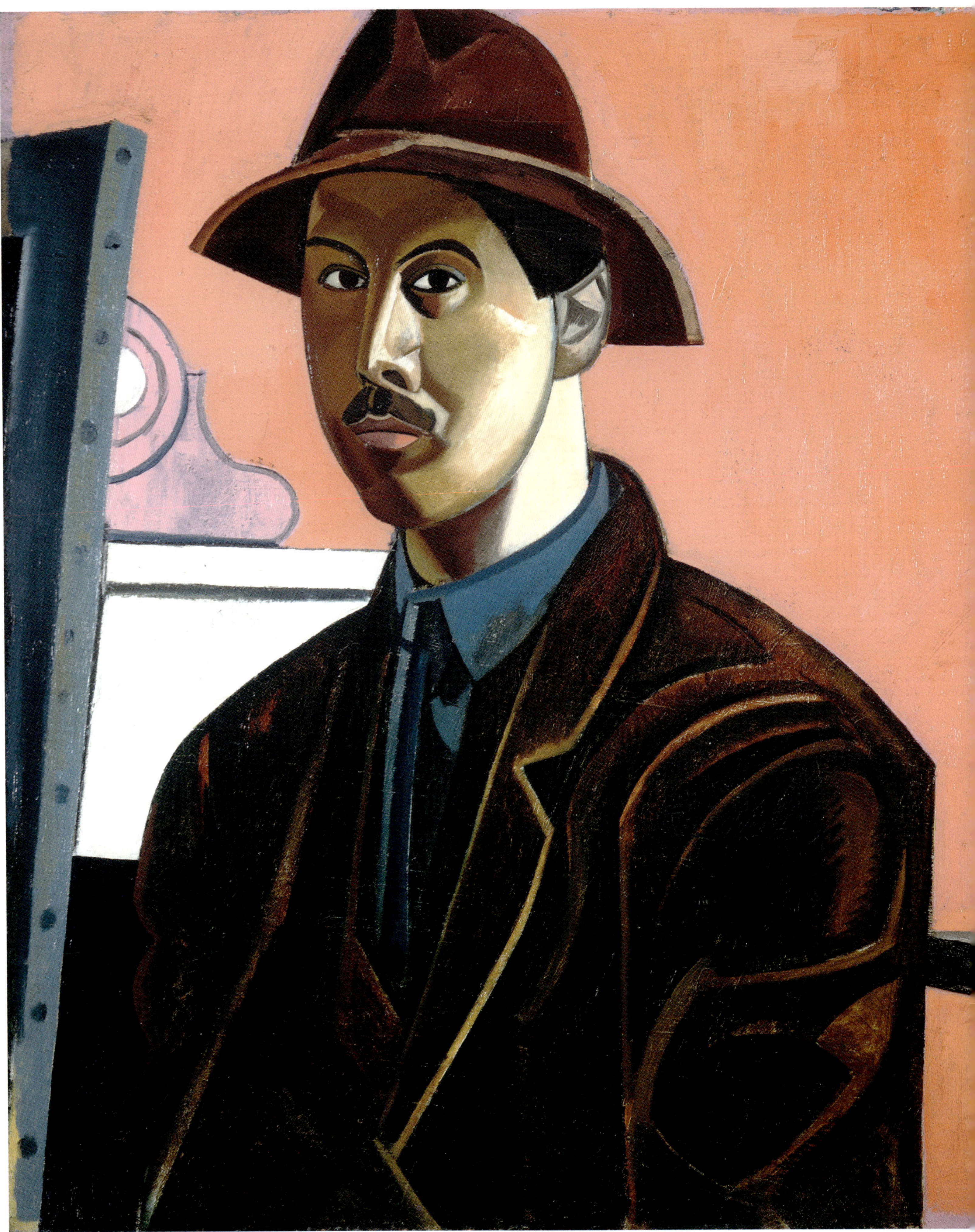

PORTRAIT OF THE ARTIST AS THE PAINTER RAPHAEL, 1921
Oil on canvas, 76.3 x 68.6 cm
Manchester Art Gallery: 1925.579

Lewis's post-war self-portrait sought to establish a lineage with the Italian Renaissance, albeit with a playful irreverence. Its irony, however, disguised a serious intent. Lewis always considered himself 'classicist' by nature, and the portrait with its mask-like features and blank stare deny any glimpse of underlying emotion or introspection. Instead, the painting's concerns lie with a cool, dispassionate rendering of external surfaces and abstract form, and serve as a statement of the artist's own perceived asceticism.

Another notable aspect of Lewis's self-portrayal is the wide-brimmed hat he wears. Hair-loss caused by influenza contracted during the great epidemic of 1918 meant he was seldom ever without his Austrian velour hat, even when indoors. This, however, became the distinguishing feature of his antagonistic 'Enemy' persona, adopted during the 1920s.

EDITH SITWELL, 1923–35
Oil on canvas, 86.4 x 111.8 cm
Tate: N05437

The 1920s saw Lewis evolve a new aspect to his art – that of portraiture. It was a move intended to attract new patrons and re-integrate himself, albeit fractiously, into British artistic and literary life after the First World War.

The aristocratic poet, Edith Sitwell, was one such acquaintance. Although no admirer of her poetry, Lewis perceived her as a possible patron, and saw in her and her writer brothers, Osbert and Sacherverell, a potential foil to the despised Bloomsbury set.

Lewis began his portrait of Sitwell in 1923, its exquisitely modelled head reflecting the qualities he saw in her – determination and self-assuredness. The portrait also captures the poet's idiosyncratic dress sense, showing her wearing a vividly coloured robe and what appears to be a turban-style hat.

Lewis and Sitwell's association cooled once it was obvious she did not possess the wealth of Osbert and Sacherverell. Lewis, also sensitive to her perceived slights, ridiculed her and her brothers in his stinging social satire, *The Apes of God*, in 1930. The relationship having broken down, Lewis finished the portrait in her absence in 1935. It is notable that Edith's hands – the only part of her which she felt to be attractive – are concealed, perhaps indicating the bitterness that now existed between them.

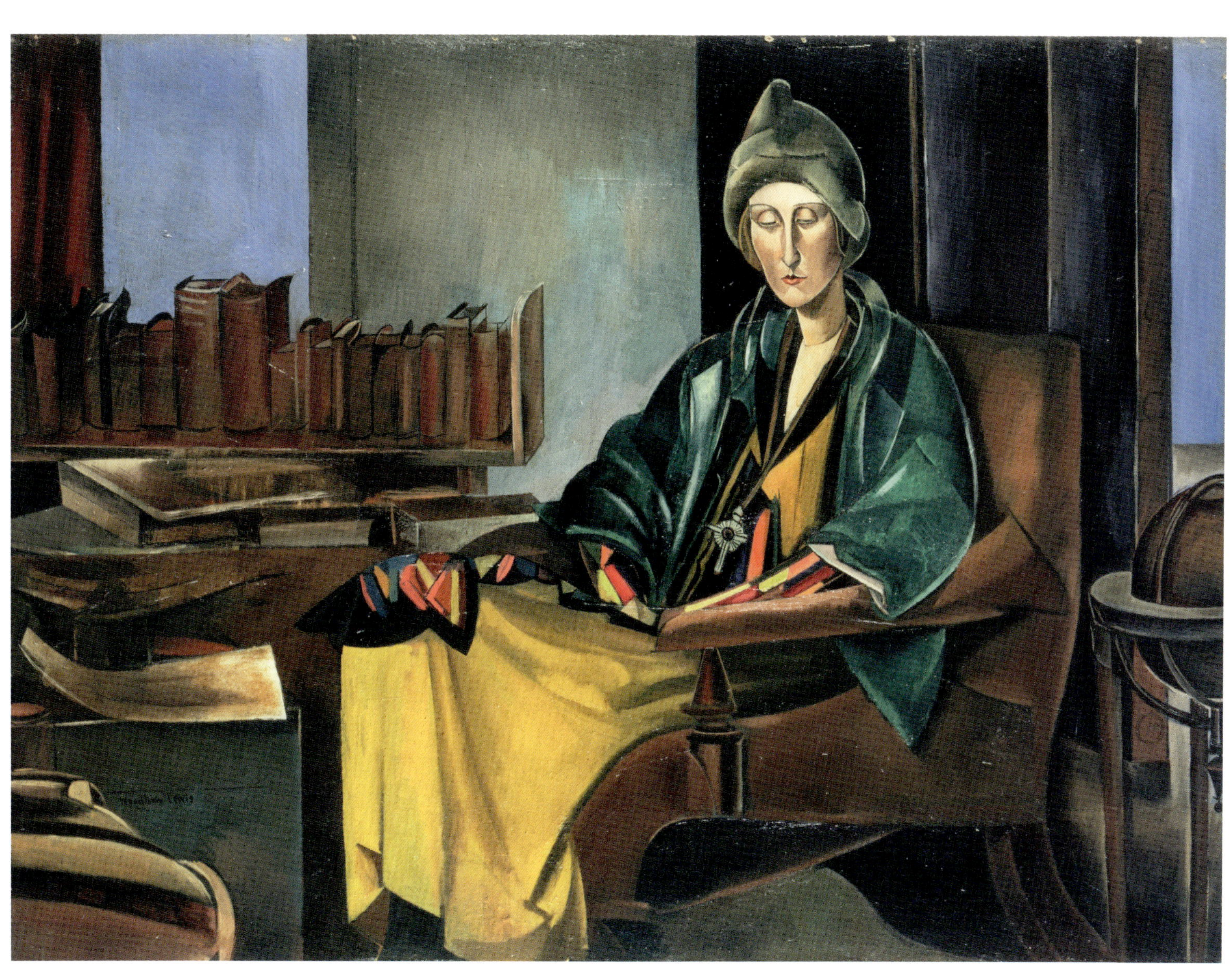

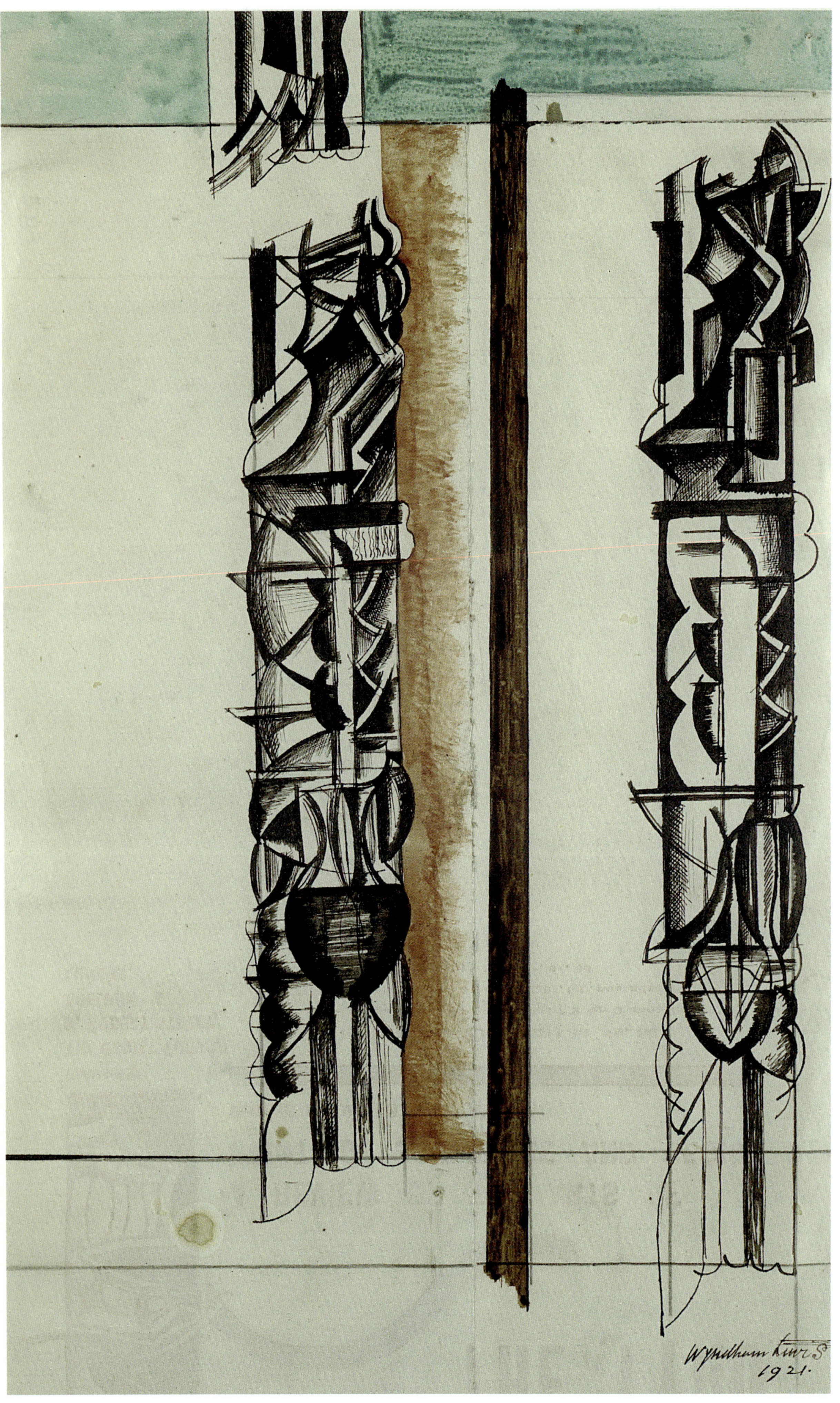
Wyndham Lewis
1921.

COLUMN FIGURES, 1921
Ink and watercolour on paper, 28.5 x 17 cm
British Council: P184

In 1919 Lewis published his thoughts for a revitalised post-war art in *The Caliph's Design*. In it, he argued that the preservation of the modernist impulse was dependent on its release 'into the general life of the community' in the form of architecture, so saving it from the stagnation of 'Cubist "natural mortism", nostalgic classicism or the passivity of Bloomsbury formalism'.

Lewis's drawing *Column Figures* retains his interest in an 'architectural' abstraction, while also injecting the influence of Middle Eastern or the so-called 'native' cultures of Africa. It results in an image of two complex, hieratic forms, that shares affinities with architectural blueprints.

The work was executed on the obverse of a sheet of notepaper with the heading of Lewis's 1921–22 magazine, *The Tyro*.

FROM THE SEA TO THE MOUNTAINS, 1934
Pen & ink and gouache on paper, 46 x 29.5 cm
British Council Collection: P137

Having visited Morocco in 1931, Lewis imbues his drawing *From the Sea to the Mountains* with the spirit of foreign travel. On first inspection it appears to be a rare example in Lewis's *oeuvre* of a straight landscape; the buildings and a moored fishing boat imply a North African or Mediterranean setting. Yet readings are fleeting. Perceptible elements such as the boat and the cloud-topped mountains, that establish a conventional foreground to the background pictorial arrangement, are undermined by features like the mysterious twin 'suns' that sit centrally within the composition.

Lewis's refusal to create a mere 'frozen moment' or a 'snapshot' vista captures an urge to generate a more cerebral image, one that reconciles fugitive recollections and illusory, perhaps contradictory, memory. Thus *From the Sea to the Mountains* provides an intriguing facet of a central theme of Lewis's art in the interwar – the juncture of the physical world and the world of the human subconscious.

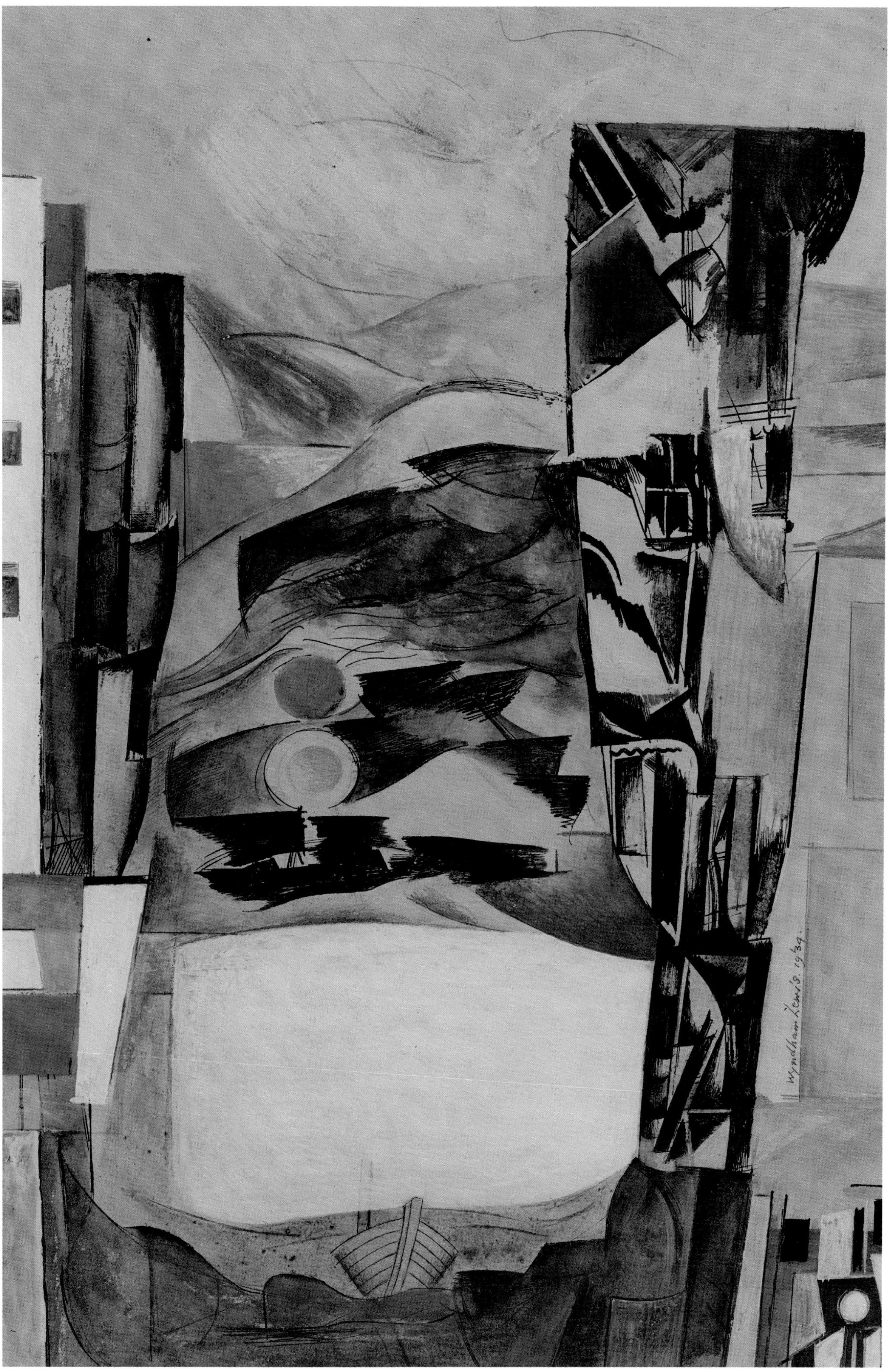
Wyndham Lewis. 1939.

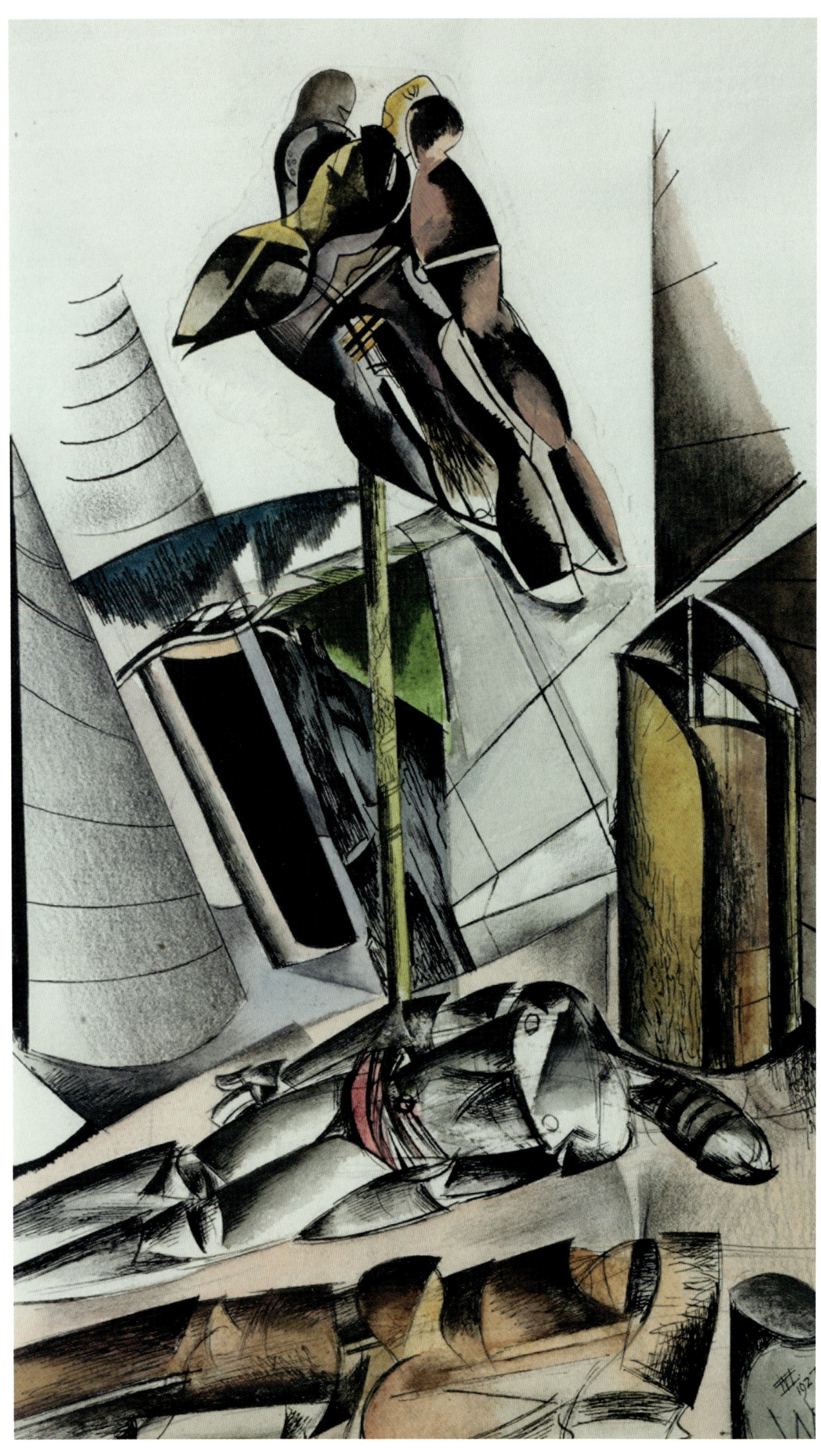

FIGURES IN THE AIR, 1927
Ink, pencil, watercolour with *papier collé*, 29.2 x 16.5 cm
Private collection

Lewis was drawn to archaic legends and fertility rites, such as those described in James Frazier's *The Golden Bough* (1890) or in stories of sacrificial kings and heroes in Celtic mythology. Some have speculated that this stemmed from an affinity Lewis felt between these and the great sacrifice of the First World War. This cannot be substantiated in *Figures in the Air*, although in the prone muscular figure impaled on a spear there is the suggestion of a ritualised killing. Lewis offers no clues either as to the beings suspended from the spear's shaft, which give the drawing its title, or the black opening at the centre of the composition, which may represent a tomb entrance or a gateway to another dimension. Instead, the viewer perceives a scene belonging to a mystic parallel realm; the inclusion of *papier collé* elements and mannequin-like figures invites comparisons with the Surrealism of Max Ernst and the 'metaphysical' art of Giorgio de Chirico .

INCA WITH BIRDS, 1933
Oil on canvas, 67.3 x 54.6 cm
Arts Council Collection: ACC4/1959

Inca with Birds belongs to the series of 24 imaginary compositions which Lewis
completed over the course of the 1930s, and like others it has a historical theme.

Fond of obscure romantic histories, Lewis was particularly inspired by the writings
of the blind American historian William H Prescott, notably his *The Conquest
of Peru* (1847) which recounted the suppression of the Incas by the Spanish
conquistadores. *Inca with Birds*, with its male figure entering water, probably depicts
the mythic Eldorado cleansing ritual or an Inca initiation ceremony of the kind
Prescott described involving the collection of exotic bird feathers. This may explain
the two tethered birds and the 'beaked' form imposed over the male initiate; this
perhaps is a ceremonial mask or representative of a transcendental experience.

Described by Lewis as 'a (non-Freudian) dream picture', *Inca with Birds*
incorporates elements of Cubism and 'metaphysical' art to conjure an unearthly
spectacle where meanings are intentionally nuanced. Even so, with its allusions
to Spanish invasion, the painting may have references to the new expansionist
regimes of the 1930s, most notably Fascist Italy.

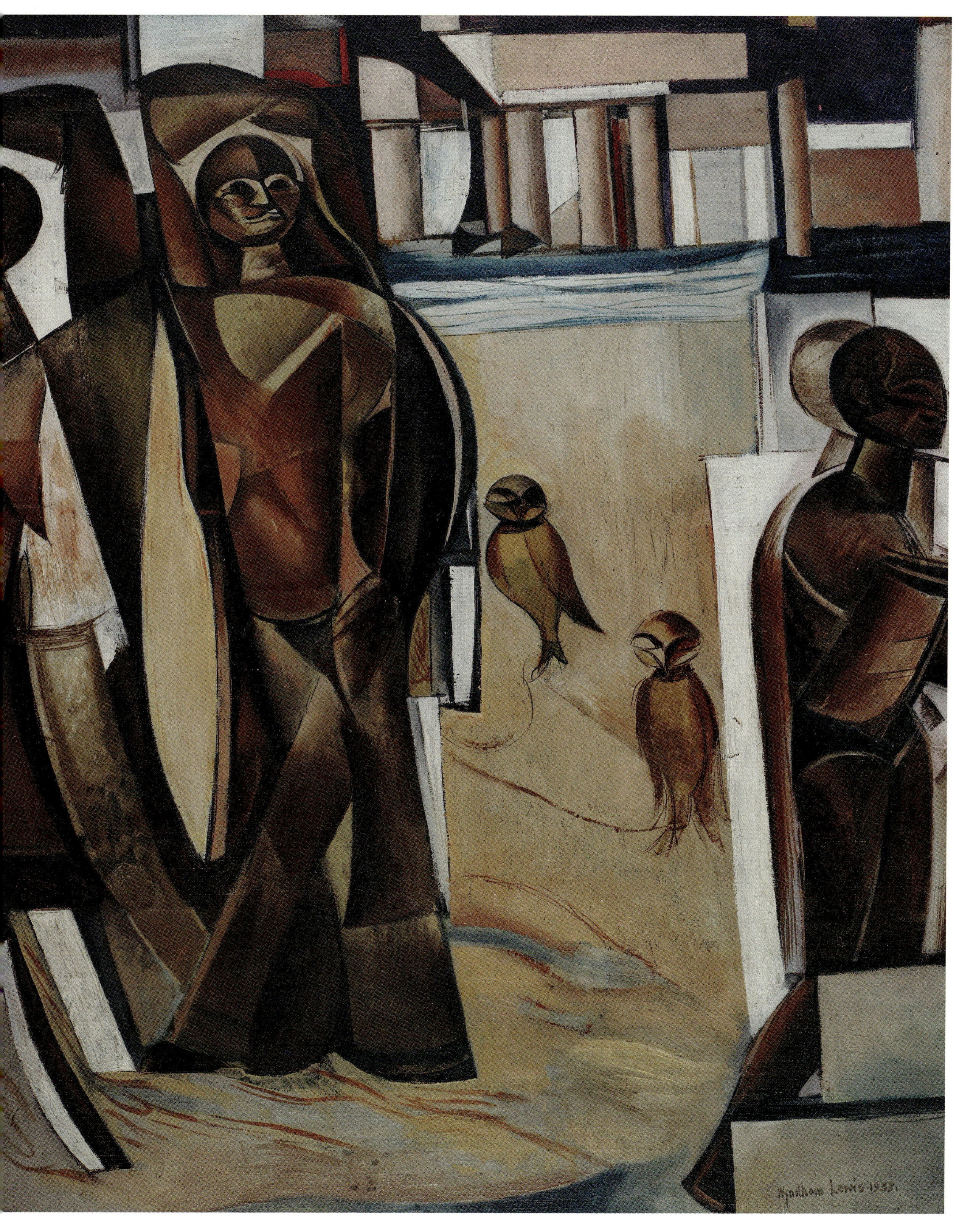

Wyndham Lewis 1933.

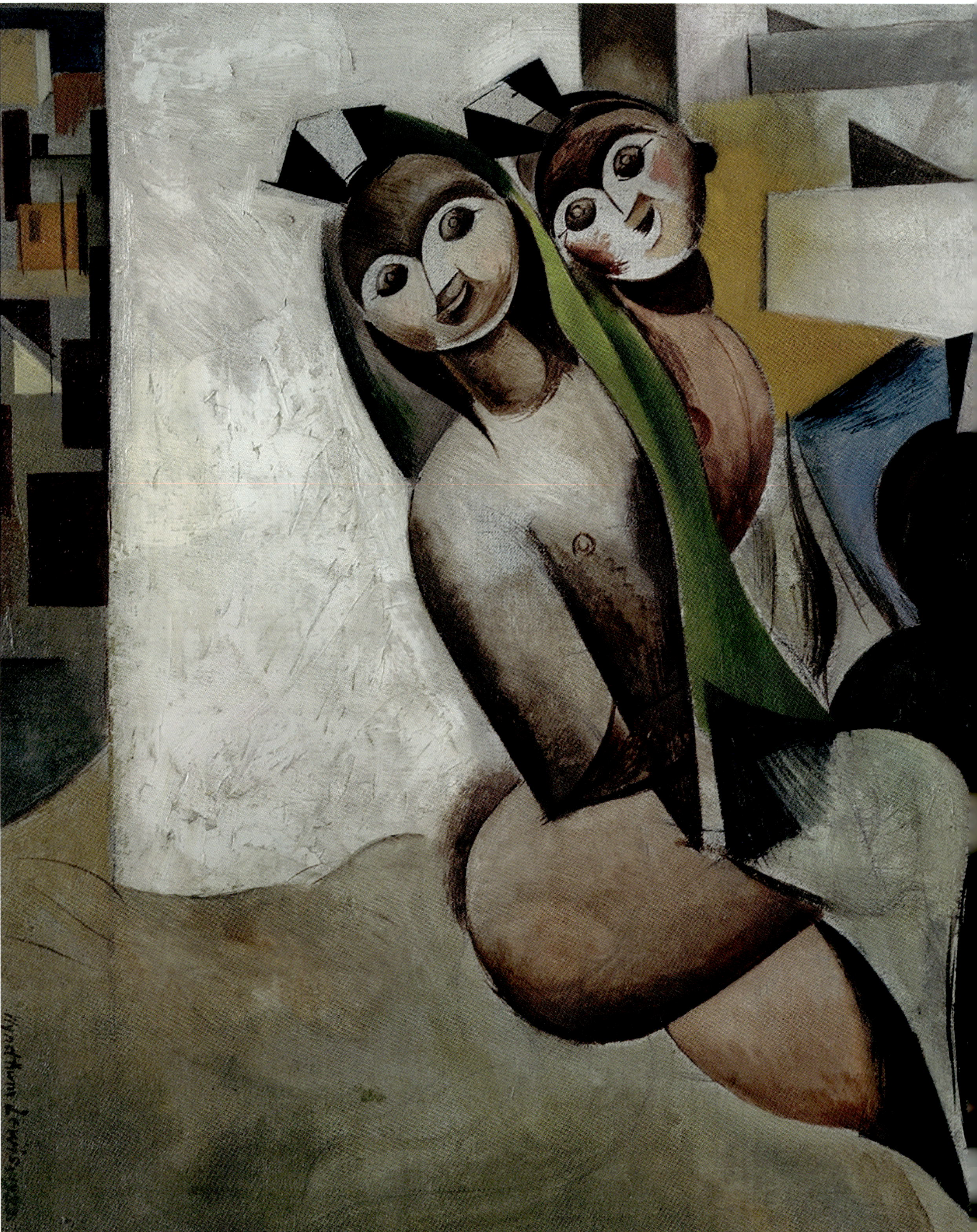

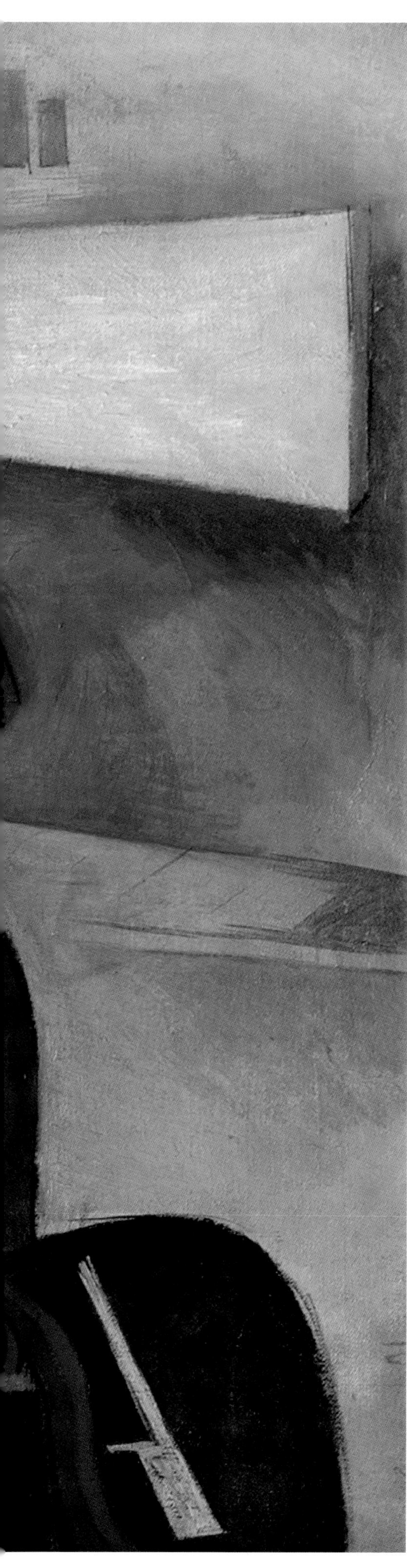

TWO BEACH BABIES, 1933
Oil on canvas, 51 x 61.5 cm
Rugby Art Gallery and Museum: RC059

Beset by poverty, ill-health and the threat of litigation for his withering satire, Lewis began painting in earnest from 1932. He eventually created a sequence of 24 paintings that formed the basis of his single-artist show – *An Exhibition of Paintings and Drawings by Wyndham Lewis* – at the Leicester Galleries in December 1937. These paintings were characterised by their historical, mythological and afterlife themes and by their eclectic mix of styles, which included aspects of Cubist and 'metaphysical' art, as well as elements of Ancient Egyptian and Chinese traditions.

Two Beach Babies is an early work from the series and sees Lewis return to a subject popular in his art – that of the beach. In keeping with Lewis's work of the period, the painting seems to feature a metaphysical realm inhabited by two imaginary female beings. The sense of a timeless seaside utopia is offset by the painting's title, a reference to the 'bathing beauties' prevalent in the tourist publicity of the day. By this, Lewis appears to muse on the sexual politics of the 1930s, and despite its imaginary subject-matter the painting serves as an intentional critique of contemporary social attitudes.

THE SURRENDER OF BARCELONA, 1936
Oil on canvas, 83.8 x 59.7 cm
Tate: N05768

At Lewis's 1937 solo exhibition at the Leicester Galleries, the most impressive canvas was *The Surrender of Barcelona* – a richly coloured and complex architectural composition. William H. Prescott was again Lewis's inspiration, this time with his *History of Ferdinand and Isabella the Catholic* (1838). The painting shows the forces of the Spanish king and queen securing their succession with the fall of the Catalonian capital in 1472.

In its theme of Spain's military and imperial past, *The Surrender of Barcelona* followed a pattern consistent with *The Armada* (pp 66–67) and *Inca with Birds* (pp 58–59). There were allusions also to its past artistic depiction, particularly Diego Velazquez's masterpiece, *The Surrender of Breda* (1635) with which it shared a similar title. This was evident too in the raised lances of the horsemen positioned right, which mimic those of Velazquez's victorious Spaniards.

Lewis stated that he wished 'to paint a Fourteenth Century scene as I should do it could I be transported there'. Even so, it is difficult to believe *The Surrender of Barcelona* was not influenced by unfolding contemporary events. While in progress the Spanish Civil War broke out in 1936 and ended with the surrender of Barcelona, a Republican stronghold, in January 1939. This may have motivated Lewis's subtle change of title from an original *The Siege of Barcelona* to *'The Surrender'*.

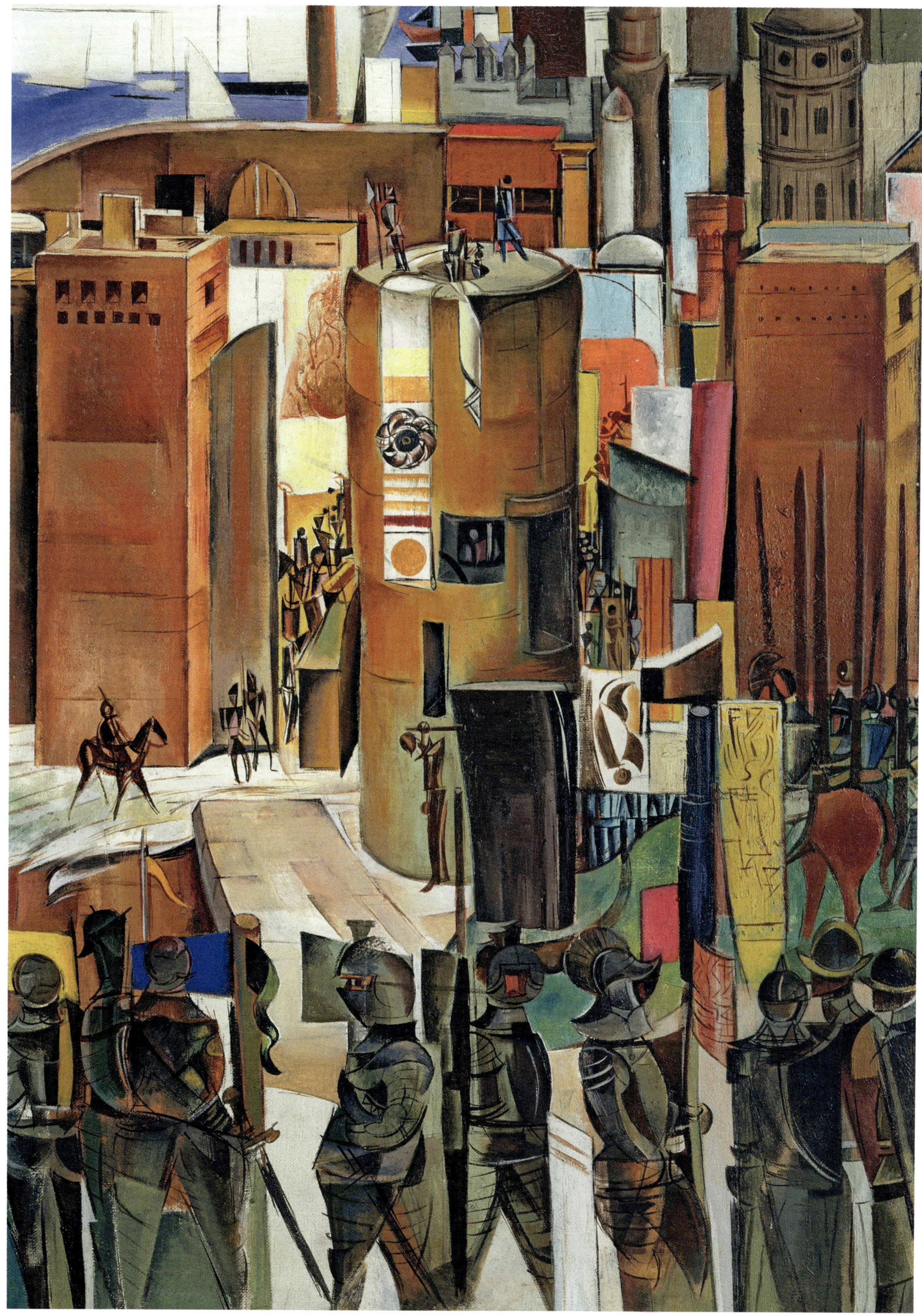

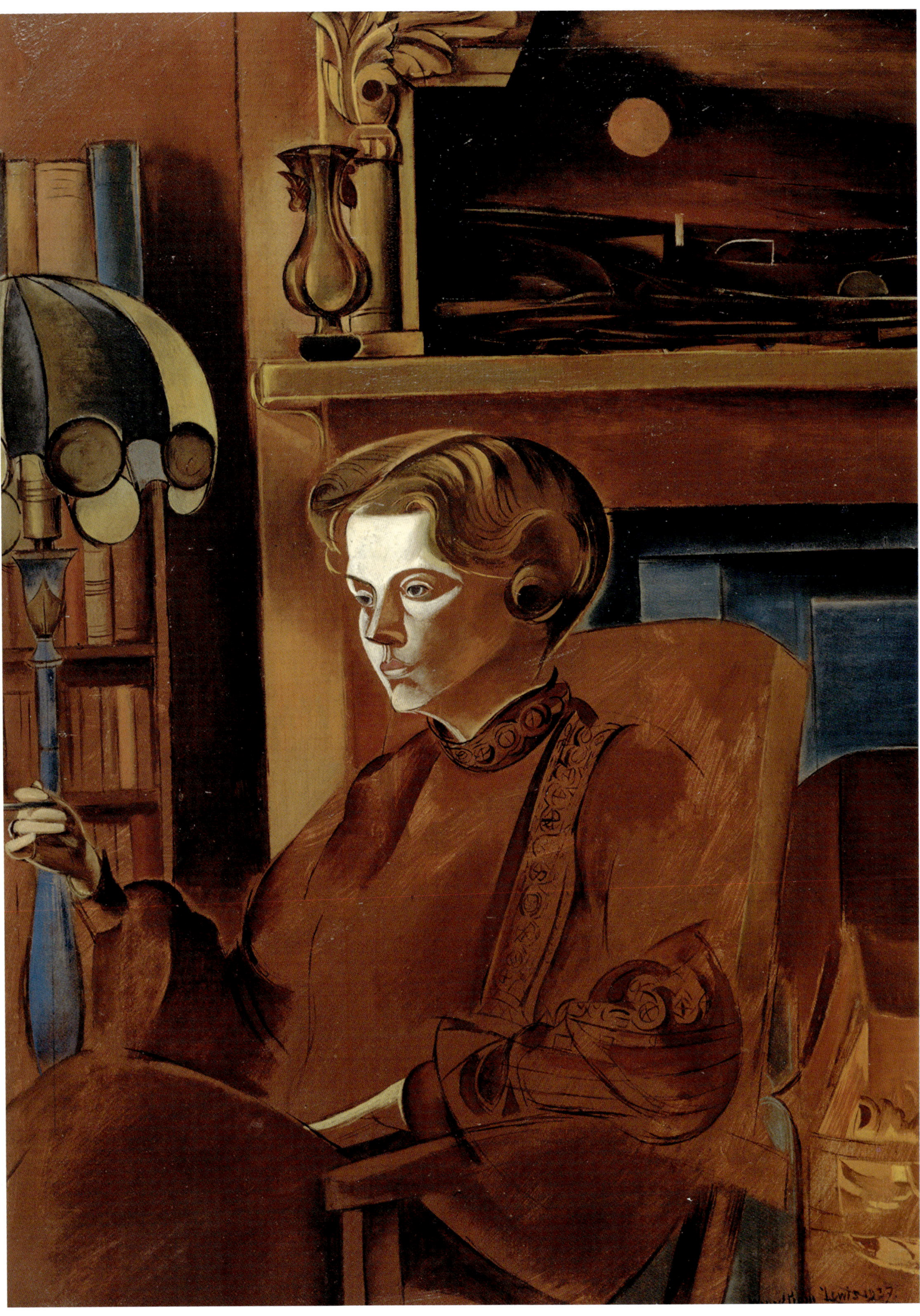
Wyndham Lewis 1937

RED PORTRAIT (FROANNA), 1937
Oil on canvas, 92 x 61.5 cm
Wyndham Lewis Memorial Trust: LP.2000.XX.1

Alongside portraits of patrons and friends, Lewis, between 1933 and 1939, painted at least five portraits of his wife, Gladys Anne 'Froanna' Hoskyns. Of these, *Red Portrait (Froanna)* is the most beguiling; in its study of consciousness it was the closest in spirit to his imaginary compositions of the same period. In the painting, Froanna appears to merge into the warm earth hues of her surroundings, a partial physical presence drifting into subconscious. This is further implied by the enigmatic landscape above the mantelpiece, whose sun motif is repeated in the lampshade design beside her, so forming a bridge between the physical world and that of the metaphysical. The portrait is partly based on the earlier drawing of *Froanna, Young Woman Seated* (1936, Wyndham Lewis Memorial Trust, bequest of Tom Rosenthal) – one of several drawings of Froanna wearing the full-sleeved blouse featured in *Red Portrait*.

   Lewis's relationship with Froanna was complex. Though she was the subject in numerous artworks, she was only ever introduced to Lewis's closest associates and was usually an unseen presence when visitors called at their home. Lewis's portraits nevertheless suggest a close bond between them. The artist was especially proud of *Red Portrait*, and was aggrieved when it was overlooked by the Institute for the Contemporary Art (ICA) for an exhibition in 1948, which instead chose the 'posterish' *Mr Wyndham Lewis as a Tyro* (1921) to represent his art.

THE ARMADA, 1937
Oil on canvas, 91.5 x 71.4 cm
Vancouver Art Gallery: VAG 51.3

The Armada and Lewis's other paintings of the 1930s marked his re-engagement with historical subjects, having previously produced two large-scale memorial canvases for the Canadian and British official war art schemes in the First World War. Unlike these earlier commissions, *The Armada* was a flight of the imagination and Lewis's handling, a highly stylised figuration, emphasised the armoured figures' presence on deck as theoretical rather than actual.

    The Armada may have depicted a past event, but it was one that had cadences with the volatile present, with tensions between Catholic Spain and Protestant England in the sixteenth century mirroring the aggressive, militarised power politics of the 1930s. However, despite its pertinence to a British audience, the implication of the subject was less one of a specific existential threat and more a broader sense of imminent momentous change.

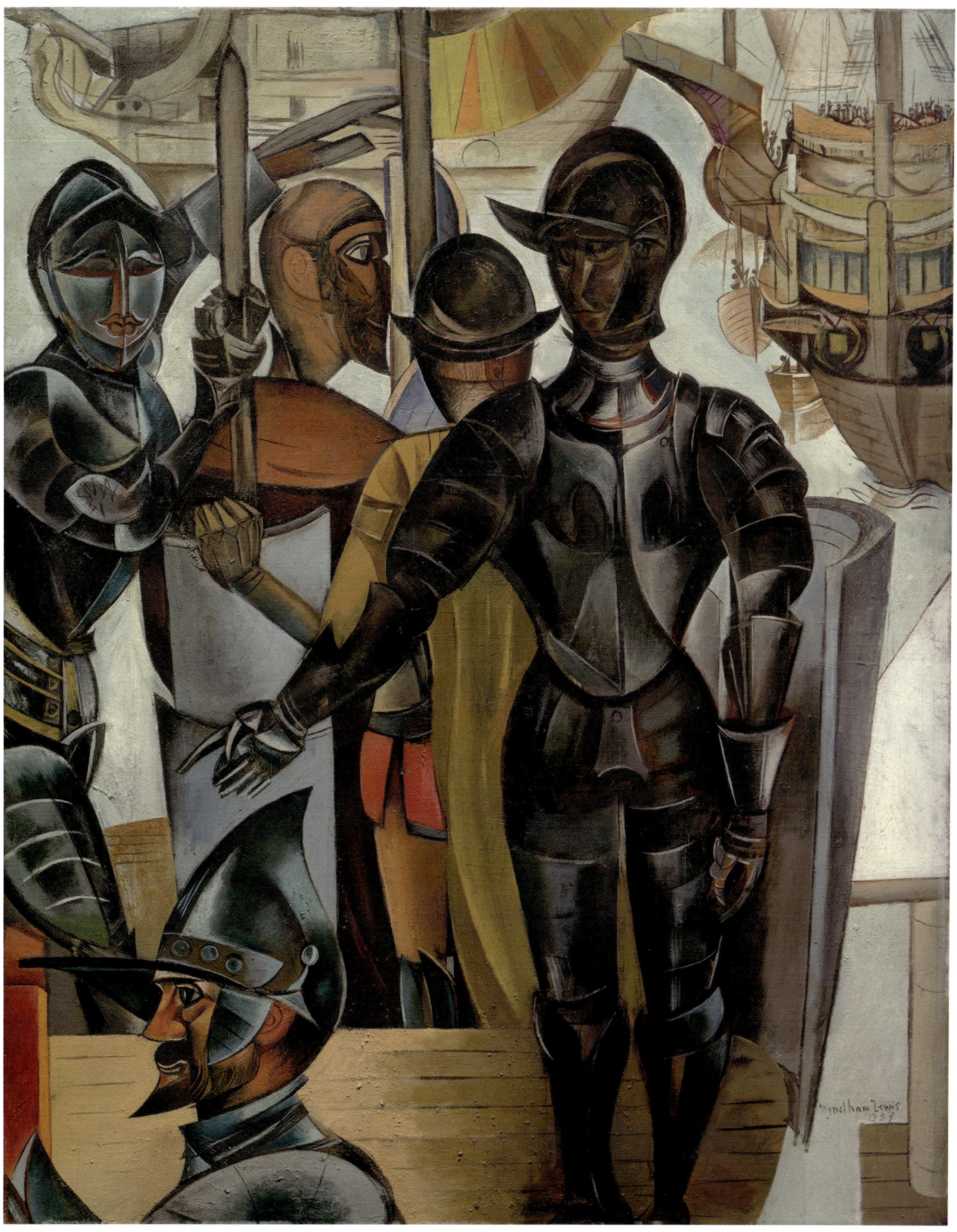

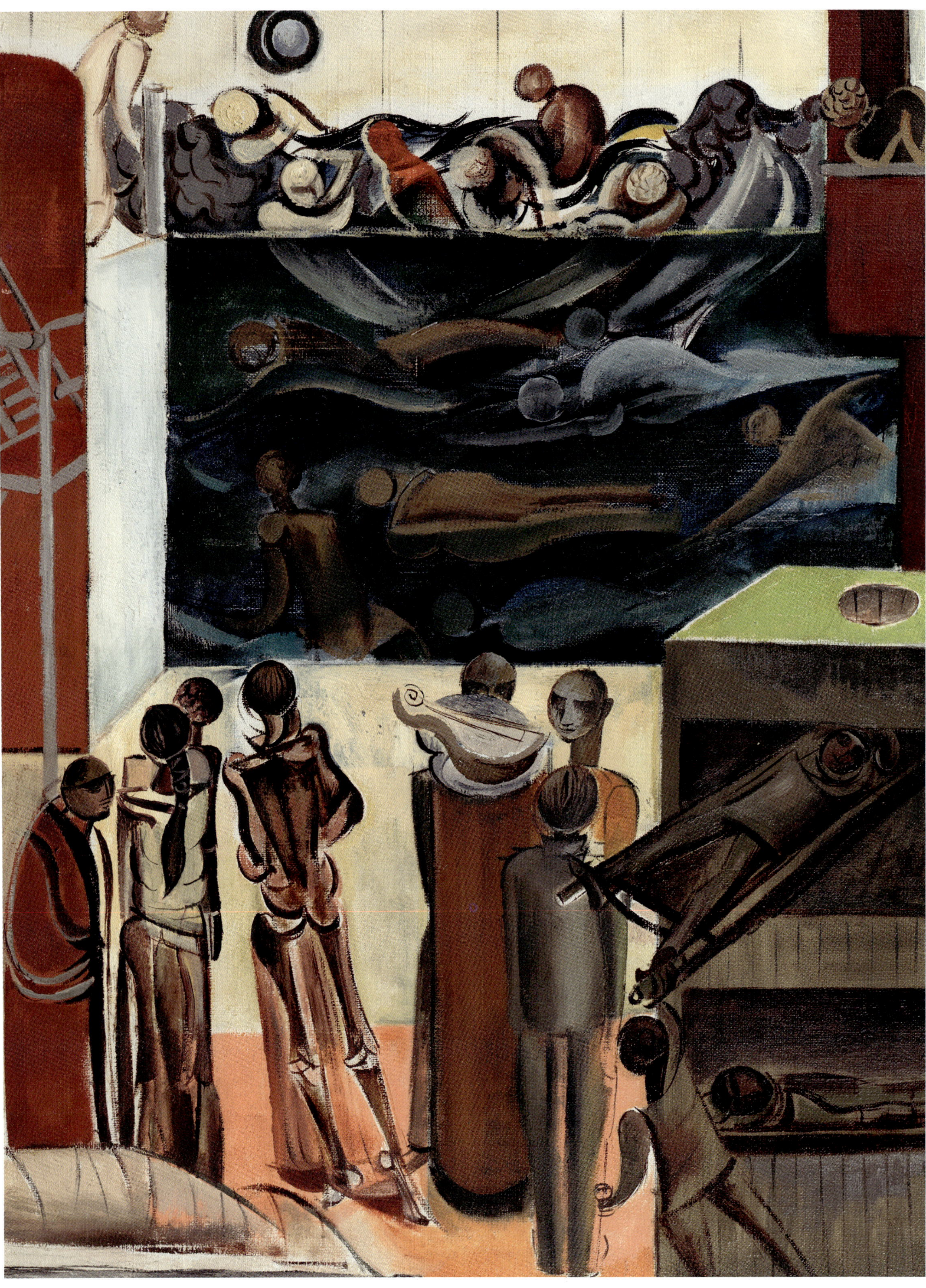

THE TANK IN THE CLINIC, 1937
Oil on canvas, 19.5 x 26 cm
Wyndham Lewis Memorial Trust: LP.2008.XX.4

Amongst Lewis's imaginative compositions of 1930s, a number, such as *The Tank in the Clinic*, dealt with the bouts of ill-health he suffered over the decade. The diagnosis for this was complex, but was rooted in venereal disease contracted before the First World War. Lewis's treatments were similarly convoluted, as inferred in the painting, which pictures a form of water therapy. As a macabre twist, Lewis adds some outlandish patients who reveal skeletal forms as they disrobe. The bathing figures seem similarly depersonalised, as if submersion has returned them to a primordial, pre-human state. In these prone forms there are close affinities with Lewis's *Inferno* (pp 72–73), painted the same year, with each painting conferring their human subjects with a collective impulse to regress or self-immolate.

NAOMI MITCHISON, 1938
Oil on canvas, 101.6 x 76.2 cm
Scottish National Portrait Gallery

Besides a series of imaginative compositions, Lewis executed a number of academic portraits in the 1930s, several of which featured sitters with whom he was acquainted.

Naomi Mitchison was a Scottish author and poet, best known now for her historical novel, *The Corn King and the Spring Queen* (1931). She and Lewis first met in 1930 and quickly became close friends. Despite Mitchison's open marriage and Lewis's notoriousl sexual appetite, their relationship seems largely to have been platonic; the artist adopted an avuncular, supportive role for the younger writer, and she supporting him during the travails and ostracism in the 1930s.

Lewis's portrait shows Mitchison in pensive mood. She was working on *The Blood of the Martyrs* (1939) at the time, and Lewis gives visual expression to her thoughts by showing her seated beside a crucifixion scene. The painting affirms Lewis's portraiture as more than just an economic necessity, and formed part of a series of psychologically charged studies of writers including Stephen Spender, Ezra Pound and T S Eliot.

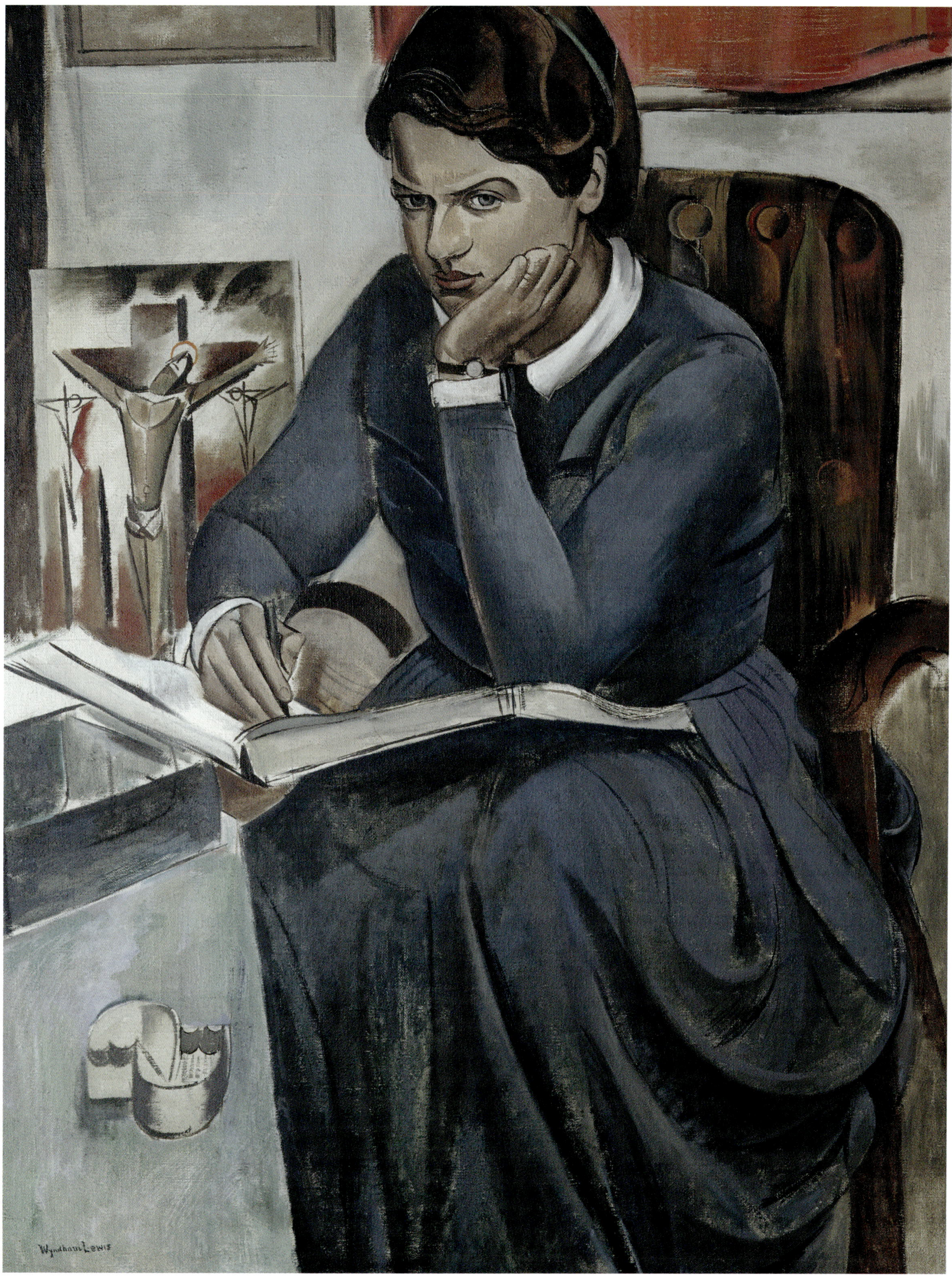

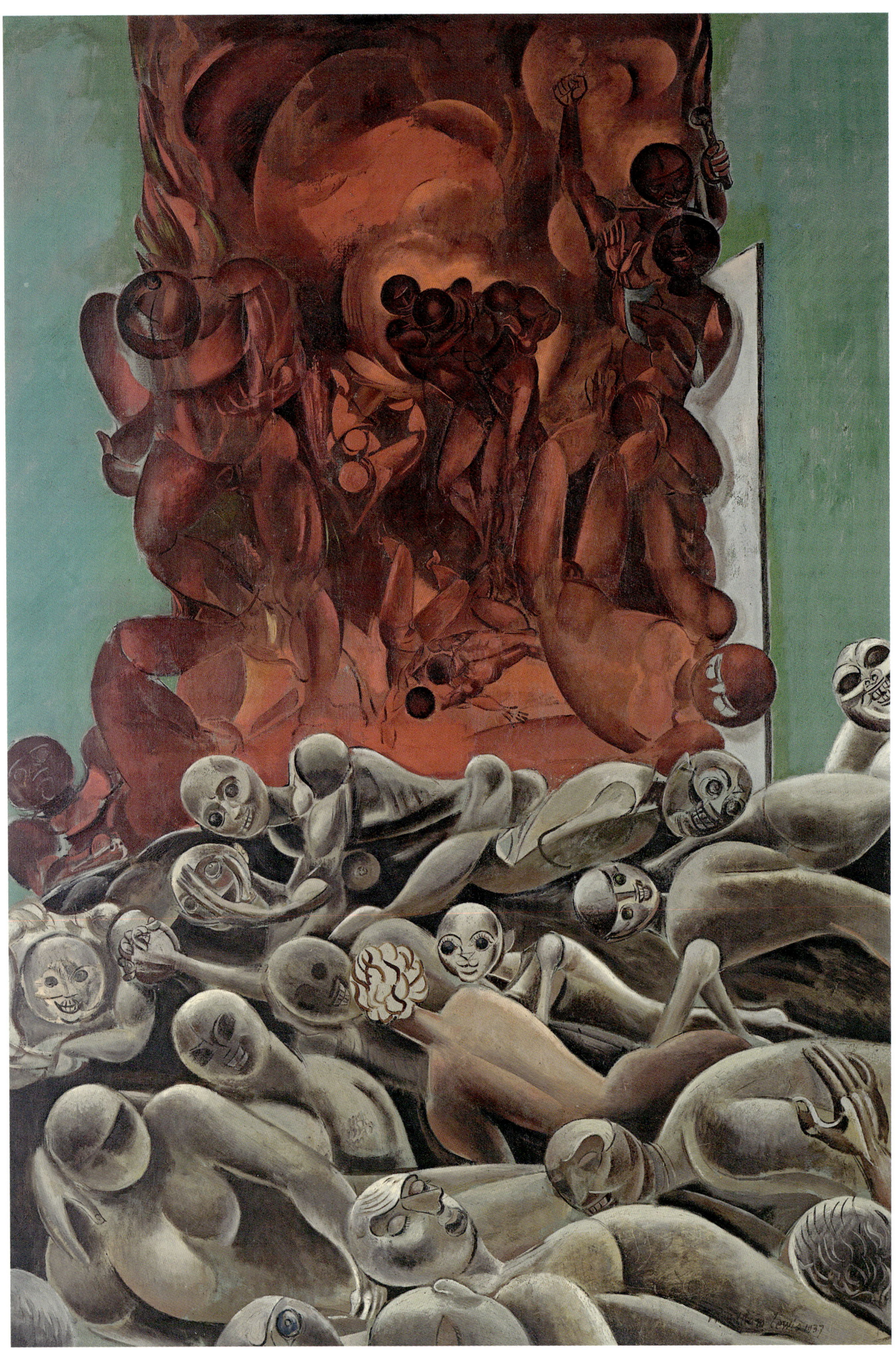

INFERNO, 1937
Oil on canvas, 152.5 x 101.8 cm
National Gallery of Victoria, Melbourne: 1411-5

Inferno was the fitting, if macabre, conclusion to the series of imaginary
compositions that Lewis made in the 1930s. The afterlife and other unearthly
planes featured in other paintings in the sequence, but none were so emphatic
in their treatment. Lewis achieved this in the bold division of its constituent parts;
'an inverted T' of a vertical molten red abyss spills forth figures into an orgiastic
horizontal grouping of prone humanoids. This Lewis described as '[a] world of
shapes locked in eternal conflict ... super-imposed upon a world of shapes, prone
in the relaxations of an uneasy sensuality which is also eternal.' Here there were
echoes of Luca Signorelli's Renaissance fresco, *The Damned Cast into Hell* (1499–
1504), a work Lewis greatly admired, though in his hell the difference between
damned and the demonic is less clear.

The painting featured in Lewis's Leicester Galleries show in 1937, where it was
exhibited still wet. Its themes of death, hell and divinity were later re-visited in art
made during Lewis's Canadian sojourn in the 1940s and in his trilogy *The Human
Age* in the 1950s. It was indicative of an overriding pessimism, the sense of a dark
core to humanity – a view undoubtedly informed by Lewis's experience of the First
World War and one that endured for the rest of his life.

T S ELIOT, 1938
Oil on canvas, 133.3 x 85. cm
Durban Art Gallery: DAG 1066

Lewis's portrait of his friend the poet T S Eliot is one of the outstanding British twentieth-century portraits. It was one of a number of psychologically charged portrayals of writers that Lewis created between 1938 and 1939. Eliot is thus presented hunched but formal, displaying his characteristic asceticism. He appears lost in thought; his gaze has drifted left. These thoughts are implied in the scrolling abstract forms situated either side of him, which serve also to undermine his mask of inscrutability.

The portrait ultimately proved Lewis's most controversial painting, owing to its surprise submission to the Royal Academy of Art's Summer Show in 1938. Lewis had always disdained the Academy, so it seemed a move calculated to fail and affirm the 56-year-old artist's continued status as a rebel. Nevertheless, the inevitable rejection caused a press furore, fuelled by Augustus John's protest resignation from the Academy.

In citing its abstract elements as the cause of the portrait's rejection, the Academy seemed to validate Lewis's contempt. Nevertheless, Winston Churchill, whom Lewis condemned a warmonger in 1936, defended the Academy's decision stating, 'the function of ... the Royal Academy is to hold a middle course between tradition and innovation ... it is not the function of the Royal Academy to run wildly after novelty'.

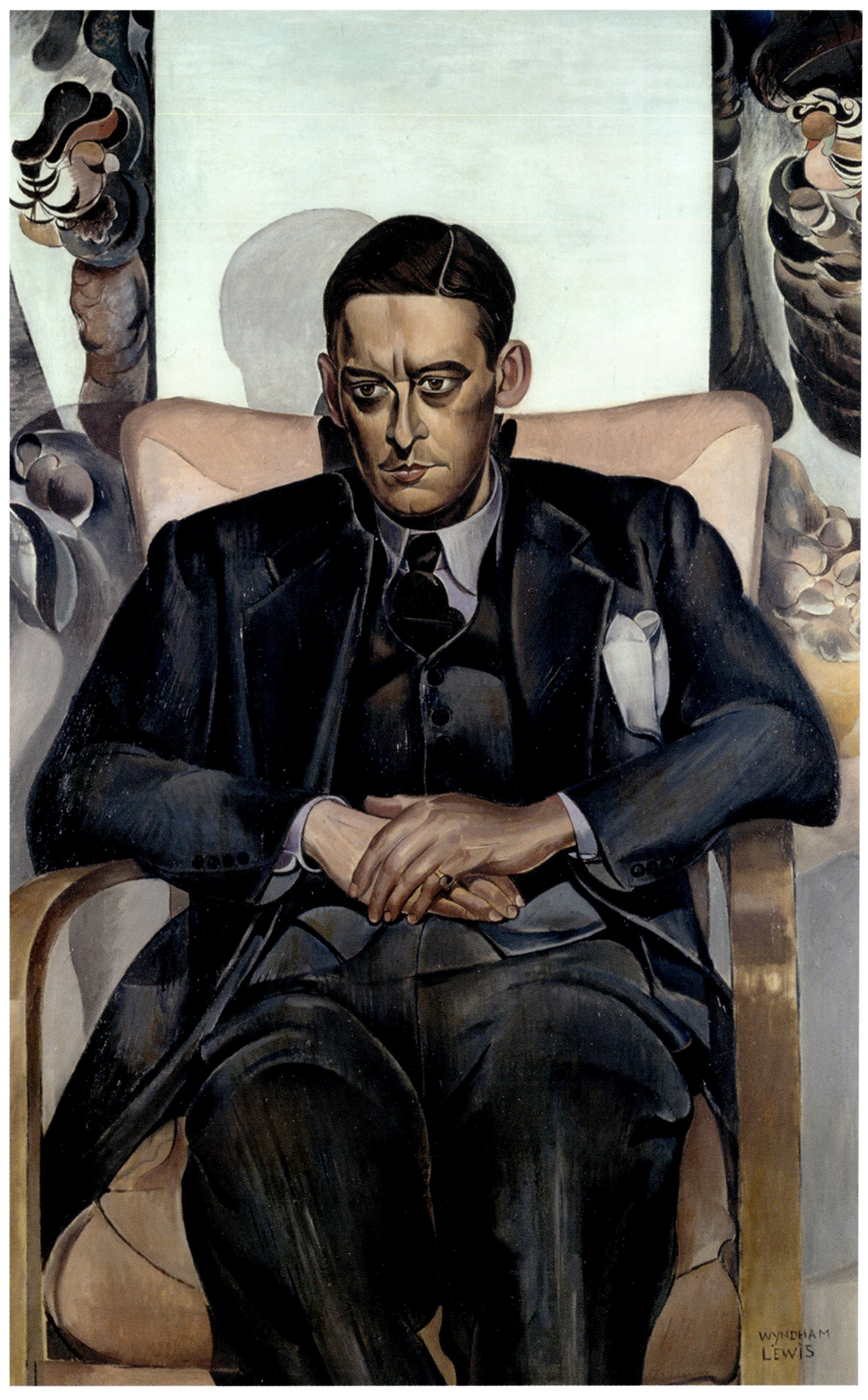
WYNDHAM
LEWIS

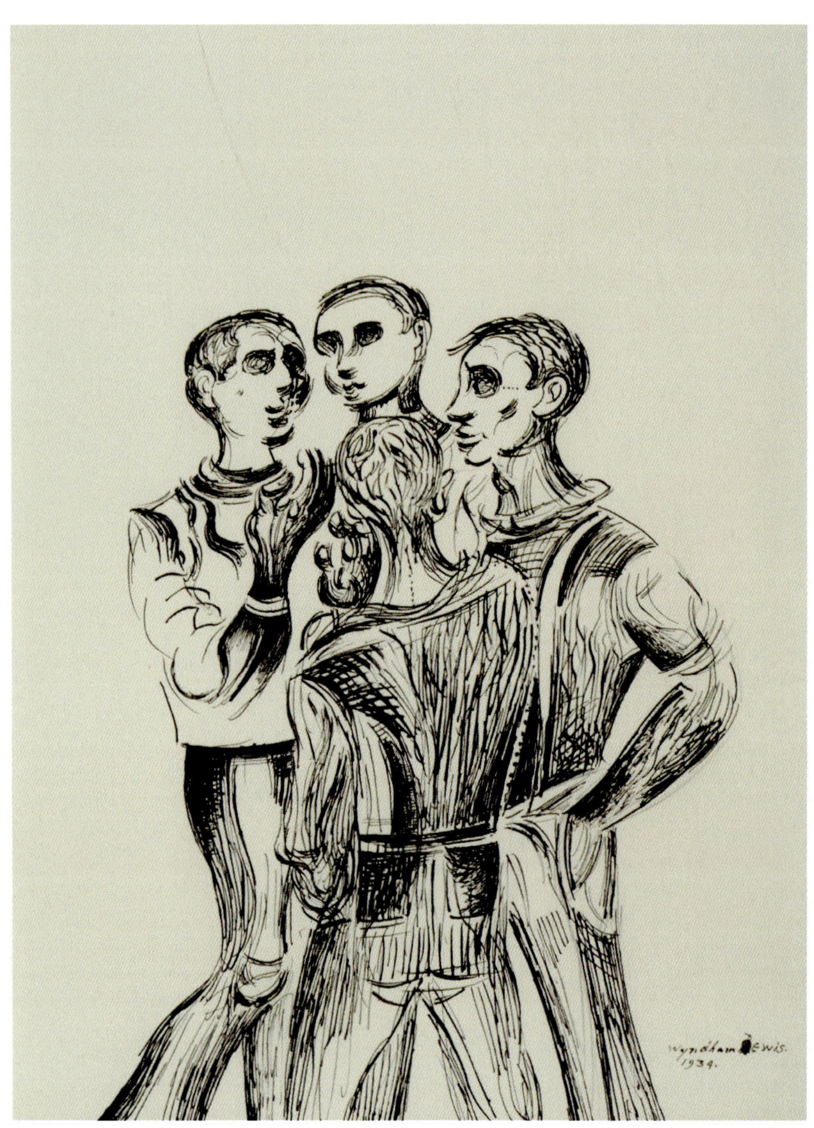

COMMUNISTS, 1930s
Ink and pencil on paper, 40 x 24 cm
Leeds Art Gallery: LEEAG.1991.0034.0016-2

Lewis was vehemently opposed to communism in the 1930s, to the extent that he was willing to support the appeasement of Adolf Hitler and other European dictators in order to halt its spread. His innate suspicion and enmity is apparent in this satirical drawing of a group of young communists. Lewis pictures them huddled conspiratorially, plotting some form of insurrectionist activity, their bare heads and workwear an affectatious display of solidarity with 'the workers'.

Lewis's anti-communism placed him at odds with many left-leaning intellectuals. To him, 'communist' sympathies within Britain's educated classes amounted to a mere 'parlour game' that refused to acknowledge the doctrine's true danger.

JEHOVAH THE THUNDERER, 1941
Pencil, ink and watercolour on paper,
37 x 25.5 cm
Wyndham Lewis Memorial Trust: LD.2010.XX.8

Lewis practised no religious faith, but he had a long interest in theological themes and the arcane knowledge of ancient religions. This peaked during his time in Canada in the early 1940s, and was expressed in numerous drawings, some of which made oblique reference to the ongoing Second World War. Most explicit of these was *Jehovah the Thunderer*. The influence of William Blake is apparent in the vengeful Old Testament God, though in the spirit of earlier theologically themed work it is presented as an inhuman deity, indistinct and turbulent, from which a jet of blue energy erupts. Or this perhaps is a flaming sword to smite the prostrate human forms before Him, emblematic of a world immersed in violence.

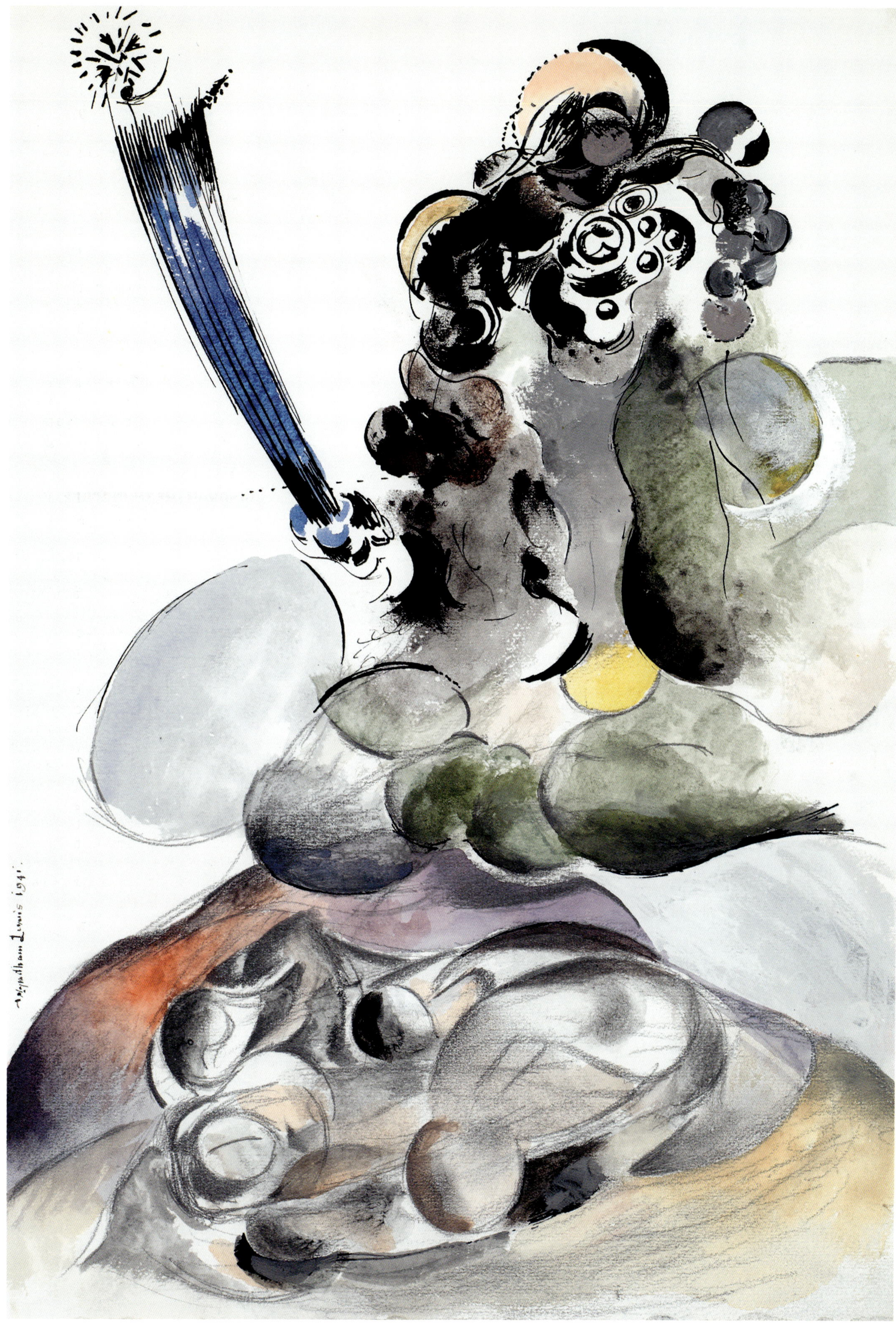

SOURCES

Preface
Kenneth Clarke letter, quoted in Jeffrey Meyers, 1980, p.273.
Mervyn Levy, 1982, p.8.

'Always on a War Footing'
Rothenstein, 1966, p.42
Lewis's Foreword to exhibition catalogue for *Guns*, 1919, quoted in Edwards 1992, p.141.

SELECTED FURTHER READING

Writings by Wyndham Lewis

(ed.) *Blast*, no.1, July 1914.
(ed.) *Blast*, no.2, July 1915.
The Caliph's Design: Architects! Where is your Vortex? London, 1919.
(ed.) *The Tyro*, no.1, April 1921.
'The Dithyrambic Spectator: An Essay on the Origins and Survivals of Art', *The Calendar of Modern Letters*,
    vol.1, no.2, April 1925, pp 89–97 (Part I); vol.1, no.3, May 1925, pp 194–213 (Part II).
The Art of Being Ruled. London, 1926.
(ed.) *The Enemy*, no. 1, January 1927.
(ed.) *The Enemy*, no. 2, September 1927.
The Lion and the Fox: The Role of the Hero in the Plays of Shakespeare. London, 1927.
Time and Western Man. London, 1927.
The Wild Body: A Soldier of Humour and other Stories. London, 1927.
The Childermass: Section One. London, 1928.
Tarr, revised edition. London, 1928.
(ed.) *The Enemy*, no. 3, March 1929.
Paleface: The Philosophy of the 'Melting-Pot'. London, 1929.
The Apes of God. London, 1930.
Blasting and Bombadiering. London, 1937.
Self Condemned, London, 1954.
The Human Age: Book One, Childermass. London, 1956.
The Human Age: Book Two, Monstre Gai; Book Three, Malign Fiesta. London, 1955.

Books and catalogues about Wyndham Lewis

Cunchillos Jaime, Carmelo (ed.) *Wyndham Lewis the Radical: Essays on Literature and Modernity.* Berne, 2007.
Edwards, Paul. *Wyndham Lewis: Art and War.* London, 1992.
Edwards, Paul. *Wyndham Lewis: Painter and Writer.* New Haven and London, 2000.
Edwards, Paul, with Richard Humphreys. *Wyndham Lewis Portraits.* London, 2008.
Farrington, Jane. *Wyndham Lewis.* London, 1980.
Fundación Juan March. *Wyndham Lewis 1882–1957.* Madrid, 2010.
Gasiorek, Andrzej. *Wyndham Lewis and Modernism.* Tavistock, 2004.
Gasiorek, Andrzej, and Nathan Waddell (eds). *Wyndham Lewis: A Critical Guide.* Edinburgh, 2015.
Gasiorek, Andrzej, Alice Reeve-Tucker and Nathan Waddell (eds). *Wyndham Lewis and the Cultures of
    Modernity.* Aldershot, 2011.
Humphreys, Richard. *Wyndham Lewis.* London, 2004.
Klein, Jacky (ed.) *The Bone beneath the Pulp: Drawings by Wyndham Lewis.* London, 2004.
Klein, Scott. *The Fictions of James Joyce and Wyndham Lewis: Monsters of Nature and Design.* Cambridge, 1994.
Levy, Mervyn. *Reflections in a Broken Mirror: Fragments of an Autobiography.* Richmond, 1982.
Mastin, Catharine, Robert Stacey and Thomas Dilworth, *'The Talented Intruder': Wyndham Lewis in Canada,
    1939–1945.* Ontario, 1993.
Meyers, Jeffrey. *The Enemy: A Biography of Wyndham Lewis.* London, 1980.
Michel, Walter. *Wyndham Lewis: Paintings and Drawings.* London, 1971.
Miller, Tyrus (ed.) *The Cambridge Companion to Wyndham Lewis.* Cambridge, 2016.
Normand, Tom. *Wyndham Lewis the Artist: Holding the Mirror up to Politics.* Cambridge, 1992.

O'Keeffe, Paul. *Some Sort of Genius: A Life of Wyndham Lewis.* London, 2000.
Rothenstein, John. *Brave Day, Hideous Night.* Hamish Hamilton, 1966.
Tate Gallery. *Wyndham Lewis and Vorticism.* London, 1956.
Wragg, David. *Wyndham Lewis and the Philosophy of Art in Early Modernist Britain: Creating a Political Aesthetic.* Lampeter, 2005.

PICTURE CREDITS

All images are reproduced by permission of The Wyndham Lewis Memorial Trust / Bridgeman Images

Arts Council Collection, Southbank Centre, London: pp 58-59
Ivor Braka Ltd, London: pp 32-33
Courtesy the British Council Collection / photo © British Council: p.53, pp 54-55
Chronicle / Alamy Stock Photo: p.14, p.15
Durban Art Gallery: p.74
Folger Shakespeare Library. Folger Art Box L677 no.41. Photo by Erin Blake: p.8
Granger Historical Picture Archive / Alamy Stock Photo: p.6
IWM: p.16, p.35, p.40, p.41, pp 42-43
Leeds Museums and Galleries (Leeds Art Gallery) UK / Bridgeman Images: p.10, p.46, p.76
Manchester Art Gallery / Bridgeman Images: p.47, pp 48-49
National Gallery of Victoria, Melbourne (Michel P72; Felton Bequest, 1964): pp 72-73
National Portrait Gallery, London: p.47
Norfolk Museums Service (Norwich Castle Museum and Art Gallery): p.39
Pictorial Press / Alamy Stock Photo: p.12, p.17
Rugby Collection at Rugby Art Gallery and Museum: pp 60-61
Scottish National Gallery of Modern Art: p.44
Scottish National Portrait Gallery: pp 70-71
Southampton Art Gallery / Bridgeman Images: p.27
©Tate, London 2017: p.37, pp 50-51, pp 62-63
Trustees of the Cecil Higgins Art Gallery (The Higgins Bedford): p.26
Collection of the Vancouver Art Gallery, Founders' Fund, VAG 51.3: pp 66-67
Victoria and Albert Museum, London: p.22, p.23, p.25, pp 28-29, p.31, p.36, p.38
Wyndham Lewis Memorial Trust: p.11, p.65, p.69, p.76
UCL Art Museum, University College London: p.20, p.21, p.34

ACKNOWLEDGEMENTS

Art Gallery of Ontario, Toronto; Arts Council Collection, London; Bristol Museum and Art Gallery; British Council Collection, London; Cooper Gallery, Barnsley Arts, Museums and Archives Service; Courtauld Gallery, London; Durban Art Gallery, Durban RSA; Bryan Ferry; Richard Gault; Glynn Vivian Art Gallery, Swansea; The Higgins, Bedford; Ivor Braka Ltd.; Lise Jaillant; Kettering Museum and Art Gallery; Graham Lane; Leeds Museums and Galleries; Manchester Art Gallery; Duncan Marks; Mercer Art Gallery, Harrogate; National Galleries of Scotland, Edinburgh; National Gallery of Victoria, Melbourne; National Portrait Gallery, London; New College, Oxford; Norfolk Museums, Norwich; Offer Waterman & Co. Ltd., London; Potteries Museum and Art Gallery, Stoke; Redfern Gallery, London; David Robinson; Rugby Art Gallery and Museum; Southampton Art Gallery; Anthony Speelman; UCL Art Museum, London; Vancouver Art Gallery; Victoria and Albert Museum, London; Gordon and Sue Vint; Nathan Waddell; Whitworth Art Gallery, Manchester; Wyndham Lewis Memorial Trust; Tate, London.

Special thanks to Professor Paul Edwards (Wyndham Lewis Memorial Trust) for his time, contributions and assistance in contacting contributors and compiling the publication.

Miranda Harrison, Stephen Long and Georgia Davies (IWM).

Emma and Thomas Slocombe — thanks long overdue.

Published by IWM, Lambeth Road, London SE1 6HZ
iwm.org.uk

ISBN: 978-1-904897-38-5

A catalogue record for this book is available from the British Library

Reprographics by Altaimage, London
Printed in Slovenia by Hatherall Associates Ltd

Every effort has been made to contact all copyright holders. The publishers will be glad to
make good in future editions any error or omissions brought to their attention.

Front cover: Design by Stephen Long, incorporating photograph of Wyndham Lewis by
an unknown photographer (Pictorial Press / Alamy Stock Photo)
Back cover: Detail from *A Battery Shelled*, 1919 (see pp 42–43)
Titlepage: Detail from *Battery Position in a Wood*, 1918 (see p.41)
Frontispiece: Detail from *Inferno*, 1937 (see p.73).